SPEAK AND READ JAPANESE

Fun Mnemonic Devices for Remembering Japanese Words and Their Meanings

Larry Herzberg

Stone Bridge Press • *Berkeley, California*

Published by
Stone Bridge Press
P. O. Box 8208, Berkeley, CA 94707
TEL 510-524-8732 • sbp@stonebridge.com • www.stonebridge.com

First printing, 2017.

Printed in the United States of America.

p-ISBN 978-1-61172-040-2
e-ISBN 978-1-61172-928-3

CONTENTS

Preface 7

Radicals and phonetics 9

Common Japanese Words 13

English–Japanese Index 115

Chart of Radicals 121

PREFACE

In studying eight foreign languages over many decades, I discovered that the best way for me to learn new vocabulary in those languages was to think of mnemonic devices, i.e., memory hooks, for each word. If I could relate the sound or meaning of a word I was trying to learn to a word in English, I had a much better chance of cementing that word in my memory.

Using mnemonic devices—or "mnemonics"—to learn new vocabulary is not so crucial for an English speaker trying to learn a Romance language, given that 60 percent of words in French, Spanish, and Italian have English-language cognates. However, in a language as different from English as Japanese, having clever ways to jog your memory is most helpful when trying to learn new vocabulary.

When I was first learning Japanese, it helped me to remember the phrase for "you're welcome," *doo itashimashite*, by thinking "**don't touch my mustache**." It was also easy to remember the word *anata* ("you") by creating my own memory hook of "there'll never be **anata (another) you**." And the Japanese verb *ikimasu* ("to go") was much easier to recall if I thought about going anywhere in winter in a northern clime being an "**icky mess**."

I don't have particularly catchy memory hooks for every single word in Japanese. And even if I did, I could never fit them all into this book. What I have done here instead is provide mnemonics for almost three hundred commonly used Japanese words that all students learn in the first year or two of studying Japanese. I hope that these will encourage you to think of your own mnemonics for the words I do not include.

I taught Japanese at the college level for over twenty years. When some years ago I anonymously surveyed nearly a hundred of my Japanese-language students as to how helpful they thought my mnemonics were, nearly all of them answered that they found them either very helpful or somewhat helpful. Only one student responded that he/she found them slightly annoying. I have, therefore, continued to use them in my teaching and hope to share them with a wider audience.

I do want to share a few words of caution about using mnemonic devices to remember vocabulary. First, these are just whimsical creations that have absolutely no etymological basis. Second, mnemonic devices, or "demonic devices" as some of my students have called them, cannot be relied upon for exact pronunciation. For that you have to try to mimic your Japanese teacher, your Japanese friends, and the native speakers in the listening exercises that you do for your class. My encouraging you to remember the word for "test," *shiken*, by thinking "***she can*** ace the test, but I can't," might help you learn the word. But "she can" is hardly an exact guide to proper Japanese pronunciation.

I have yet to encounter another Japanese teacher who uses mnemonics to help students remember Japanese words. Most likely that is because most Japanese-language teachers are native speakers of the language. They have been listening to and speaking in Japanese from the time they were infants and see no reason why anyone would need tricks to learn words that they acquired with their mother's milk. A non-native speaker like me who learned the Japanese language as an adult, however, understands well the difficulty of remembering words in a language that is so incredibly different from English.

In addition to the mnemonics I have provided for spoken words, I have provided mnemonics for the kanji (Japanese characters) for those words as well. There are Chinese etymological texts that give the true origin of at least some kanji. There are other books that give tricks for remembering kanji in creative ways that have nothing to do with their actual origin. In this book I have tried to provide both the correct etymology, should that be known, as well as my own fun and hopefully helpful tricks for remembering how to read and write the kanji. The explanations of the true etymology of kanji are generally based on those found in the *Shuowen Jiezi* (説文解字), a 2nd-century Han-dynasty Chinese dictionary.

The Japanese words included in this book are ordered alphabetically based on their spelling in roomaji. The romanization used is the Hepburn system, the system most commonly used in Japanese-language textbooks for English speakers. I have, however, opted to show double vowels by writing the vowel twice, rather than using a macron (ō). For example, the long vowel "o" (おう) is thus rendered here as "oo."

Every Japanese word in the main entry is rendered in roomaji, kanji, and hiragana, except kanji are not provided for words for which there are either no kanji or for which kanji are no longer commonly used.

The English definitions of Japanese words are based on the most common meanings of those words and conform with the definitions given in the most commonly used textbooks in Japanese-language classes in the U.S., most notably the Genki series of textbooks published by Japan Times.

The mnemonic device offered for each Japanese word directly follows the English definition. For verbs the mnemonic is sometimes based on the dictionary form of the verb and sometimes on the *-masu* form. For adjectives, the mnemonics are for their root forms.

Radicals and phonetics

Every kanji contains at least one "radical," which is a simple picture that helps to show the general meaning of that kanji.

For example, the "water" radical 水, usually stylized as 氵 and placed on the left side of a kanji, is found in almost all words that are either bodies of water (河 "river"; 湖 "lake") or that have something to do with water, such as the character 渇 for "thirsty."

The "tree" radical 木 is found in almost all kanji that are either names of trees (松 "pine") or words for things made of wood (椅 "chair"). The radical is often found on the left side of a kanji, but sometimes appears on the right side, the top, or the bottom. There are 214 radicals in all, 100 of which account for nearly 99 percent of all kanji.

Approximately 90 percent of kanji currently in use also contain another type of pictograph that gives a hint as to the pronunciation of the kanji. These are called "phonetics." They are often kanji by themselves but can be written as parts of more complex kanji to help give the reader a clue to the pronunciation, at least when the kanji use the "onyomi" (Chinese pronunciation) in words composed of two or more kanji in combination. For example, the kanji that means "wash" is 洗. It's pronounced *sen* in combination with other kanji, such as in the word for "laundry" 洗濯 (*sentaku*). 洗 contains the kanji 先 that means "first," also pronounced *sen* in kanji combinations such as 先生 (*sensei*, "teacher"), and serves as a phonetic clue to pronunciation.

Part of the brilliance of kanji is that phonetics often contribute to their meanings, as well as give a clue to pronunciation. For example, the kanji 新, pronounced *atara* in the word for "new," 新しい (*atarashii*), is pronounced *shin* when it's used in combination with other kanji. This character has the "axe" radical 斤 on the right, showing the handle on the bottom right and the blade of the axe on the top and left side. The actual idea was that in order to make a new home you have to hew wooden beams with an axe. The phonetic on the left, used notably also in the first kanji in the word for "relatives," 親戚 (*shinseki*), seems to contribute to the meaning. It is written with the kanji 立 meaning "to stand" on the top, and the kanji 木 for "tree" on the bottom.

When you use an axe to make a **new** home for yourself, you must first cut down the trees standing there to clear a space.

* * *

I hope this slim volume will serve as a good supplement to whatever other resources you are using to learn Japanese. I also hope that you will continue to study a language so vital for Americans, Canadians, and other Westerners to learn. Japan is not only the world's number three economy, but a fascinating and beautiful culture with much to offer the world.

Larry Herzberg
Professor of Asian Languages
Director of Asian Studies
Calvin College
Grand Rapids, Michigan

COMMON JAPANESE WORDS

ai 愛 / あい love

*Sometimes you **eye** somebody and fall in love with them, and then **ay, yay, yay** the consequences!*

愛 The kanji shows a hand on top reaching in for someone's heart, the character 心, through a roof. This roof is the metaphoric barrier we all keep around our hearts for fear of getting hurt. The person whose love is being sought reciprocates by offering up their heart with both hands to the hand reaching in for love.

ame 雨 / あめ rain

***Ah, me**! Oh, my! It's raining!*

雨 The top horizontal line of the kanji shows the sky, with rain drops pelting down from a cloud.

anata あなた you

*There will never be **anata** you!*

Formal word for "you."

aoi 青い / あおい blue

*When sailors sail the deep blue seas and spot land, they shout "**aoi**" (**ahoy**)!*

青 This kanji is a general color word that originally meant everything from "green" to "indigo." On the top of the kanji is a plant coming out of the ground, symbolizing the color green. The bottom part, written exactly like the moon, was originally written with the kanji 丹. It shows a crucible in which the red metal cinnabar was placed in an attempt to create the elixir of immortal life in ancient times. In Japanese this kanji is now only used to mean the color "blue."

arau 洗う / あらう (to) wash

When things go ***awry*** *and you get dirty, you need to wash.*

洗 The kanji has the "water" radical 氵 on the left, logically enough. The phonetic on the right side, pronounced *sen* in *sentaku* (洗濯 "laundry"), is the *sen* in *sensei* (先生 "teacher"). 先 looks a bit like a person carrying a bath towel into the bathroom to wash up.

asa 朝 / あさ morning

Lots of us feel like ***asses*** *in the morning, before we've had our coffee!*

朝 The kanji has the "moon" radical on the right, since the moon is sometimes still visible in the sky when early morning comes. The phonetic on the left contributes to the meaning by showing the sun (日) coming up over the horizon.

ashi 足 / あし foot/feet

When you walk on a bed of hot coals, you'll get ***ash*** *on your feet.*

足 The bottom part of the kanji shows the foot in motion, with the heel and sole of the foot raised on the bottom left. The little box on top portrays the contour of the leg, although it looks like the kneecap.

ashita 明日 / あした tomorrow

From the ***ashes*** *of today comes tomorrow.*

Literally: "bright-day."

明 This kanji means "bright." It has the "sun" on the left and the "moon" on the right. Both of these heavenly bodies appear as bright lights in the sky. Tomorrow is the bright day of promise to come.

日 This kanji means "the sun" as well as "day." It was originally a circle with a dot in the middle, indicating the sun, the rising and setting of which divides day from night.

atama 頭 / あたま head

The head is composed of billions of ***atoms****.*

頭 The kanji has the "head" radical 頁 on the right, as you might expect. The phonetic on the left shows a ritual cup or other vessel, with the top line being the lid, the box below it representing the mouth of the cup, and the bottom three lines the base of the cup.

atarashii 新しい / あたらしい new

Atari *continues to produce new video games.*

新 This kanji has the "axe" radical 斤 on the right, showing the handle on the bottom right and the blade of the axe on the top and left side. In order to make a new home for yourself, you have to hew wooden beams with an axe. The phonetic on the left, used notably in the kanji 親, meaning "relative," seems to contribute to the meaning. It is written with the kanji 立 meaning "to stand" on the top, and the kanji 木 for "tree"on the bottom. When you use an axe to make a new home for yourself, you must first cut down the trees standing there to clear a space.

au 会う / あう (to) meet

*Should you bump into someone when you meet, you'll probably say "****ow!****"*

The kanji seems to show two noses (云) meeting under a roof.

basho 場所 / ばしょ location; place

*We always need to know at what place a birthday **bash** will take place.*

Literally: "field-place."

場 This kanji means "field" or any large plot of land. It appropriately enough has the earth radical on the left. The phonetic on the right shows the sun shooting down its rays on the ground.

所 This kanji has the "doorway" radical 戸 on the left, which is a separate radical created by just borrowing the left half of the "gate" radical 門 and distorting it a bit. The right side of 所 shows an axe (斤). In ancient times you had to use an axe to carve out a doorway as you built a place for your family to live.

beki da べきだ should

*You should always **bake dough** and never eat it raw.*

benri 便利 / べんり convenient

*Uncle **Ben's rice** is very convenient, since it cooks up so fast.*

Literally: "convenient-benefit."

便 This kanji means "convenient." It has the "person" radical 亻 on the left, since we humans are always looking for more convenient ways to do things. The right side shows a messenger striding along (史) carrying a bundle or package of some kind. It's certainly more convenient to have someone else carry a heavy burden for you than to do it yourself.

利 This kanji means "benefit" or "advantage." It is composed of two radicals, namely the "grain" radical on the left and the "sword" radical 刂 on the right. The actual etymology is that when you cut down the grain with a sharp instrument like a scythe, you reap the benefits.

binboo 貧乏 / びんぼう poor

*That **bimbo** is really poor after she lost her modeling career.*

Literally: "poor-lacking."

貧 This kanji has the kanji 分 on top, which shows a knife 刀 cutting something into two parts, as depicted by the two lines at the top. On the bottom of 貧 is the "money" radical 貝. If you divide up the little money there is, you will be poor.

乏 This kanji means "to be lacking." It shows a hand on top pulling out a plant on the bottom, creating the idea of taking something away.

booshi 帽子 / ぼうし cap; hat

*The red **bow she** wears on her hat is pretty cute.*

帽 This kanji means "hat." It has the "cloth" radical on the left, which originally showed a flag on a flagpole. The right side has the sun on top (日) and the eye under it (目). The idea was that a hat is something made of cloth that helps keep the sun out of your eyes.

子 This kanji, which shows a child in swaddling clothes, is a common suffix for nouns in Chinese and does not contribute to the meaning.

bunka 文化 / ぶんか culture

*To some ignorant people, culture is just a lot of **bunk**.*

Literally: "language-transformation."

文 This kanji shows a series of lines representing written language.

化 This kanji shows a person standing on the left and sitting on the right, changing position and thereby symbolizing transformation. The two kanji in combination convey the idea of the transforming power of a written language in creating civilization and culture.

bunpoo 文法 / ぶんぽう grammar

*Grammar is the big speed **bump** in the study of any language!*

Literally: "language laws."

文 This kanji shows a series of lines representing written language.

法 By itself this kanji means "law" or "way." The kanji shows water on the left and the kanji 去, meaning "to go," on the right. The true etymology of this word comes from the Chinese belief that just as water runs in certain channels, human behavior should be guided in certain channels by the rule of law. The two kanji in combination literally mean "language laws," i.e., grammar.

byooin 病院 / びょういん hospital

*You may smell a lot of **BO** (body odor) in a hospital!*

Literally: "disease-courtyard."

病 This kanji means "sickness; illness." The right side looks like a person enclosed in a room wearing a nightcap. The left and top parts of the kanji show the body as a structure that houses us, with a roof and sidewall. The two little skewed lines on the far left show germs assailing the body. In reality, the kanji has the "sickness" radical on the left, which some of my students describe as a bed, with the two feet of the patient sticking out on the far left and a hot water bottle on the very top. 丙, the phonetic on the right, shows an axe-head turned upside down.

院　This kanji means "courtyard." The radical ⻖ on the left is the outline of a mound of earth piled up, in this case to make the walls of a courtyard or compound. The phonetic on the right is the kanji "to finish." It has the "roof" radical on top. As the 2nd-century etymological text *Shuowen Jiezi* explains, in finishing the building of a house you put on the roof. Under the roof, as the phonetic for the phonetic, is the kanji 元, meaning "primordial; original." The horizontal lines symbolize the rising up out of nothingness of something being created from a primordial state. However, it looks like the legs of a person, showing from under a hospital gown. Hopefully the patient will return to his or her original state of health after being in the hospital.

byooki　病気 / びょうき　sick; ill

*Sometimes **BO** (body odor) is a clue that you may be sick.*

Literally: "sick-air."

病　This kanji means "sickness; illness." The right side looks like a person enclosed in a room wearing a nightcap. The left and top parts of the kanji show the body as a structure that houses us, with a roof and sidewall. The two little skewed lines on the far left show germs assailing the body. In reality, the kanji has the "sickness" radical 疒 on the left, which some of my students describe as a bed, with the two feet of the patient sticking out on the far left and a hot water bottle on the very top. 丙 is the phonetic on the right, which actually depicts an axe-head turned upside down.

気　This kanji, meaning "air," shows air rising (气) from a certain place (〆).

chichi　ちち　my father [humble]

***Chee, chee**, go the chimps. Monkeys, according to Darwin, are the father of us all. [O.K., a distortion of Darwin, but we're after a mnemonic device here!]*

父　This kanji, which by itself means "father," shows the father's two hands raised above his head in a gesture of authority.

chiisai　小さい / ちいさい　small; little

*Little pieces of **cheese** are just the thing to catch mice.*

小　The kanji actually shows a person with arms at their side, looking small.

chikai　近い / ちかい　near; close

*You have to be near to your dance partner to dance **cheek** to **cheek**.*

近　The kanji has the "walk" radical 辶 on the left. The phonetic on the right, an axe, contributes to the meaning. It refers to ancient combat, in which the warrior had to get close enough to his enemy to hew him with an axe.

chotto　ちょっと　a little ... [adverb]

*It's always fun to have a little **chat** with a friend.*

chuumon　注文 / ちゅうもん　order (something)

*We order something in a restaurant so we'll have something to **chew on**.*

Literally: "annotating-language." Often used with *suru*.

注　This kanji has the "water" radical 氵 on the left. On the right, as a phonetic, is the kanji 主, meaning "ruler." The ruler in ancient China was a king 王 who rose like a flame above his people, visible to all. The top stroke is the flame. 注 means "to annotate," i.e., to make a note of something. The ruler and his officials were responsible for managing and making a record of canals, irrigation projects, etc.

文 This kanji shows a series of lines representing written language.

These two kanji in combination came to mean "to order something by making a note of something in writing."

chuushoku 昼食 / ちゅうしょく lunch

Japanese ***chew shocking*** *things for lunch sometimes, including octopus and squid!*

Literally: "noon-food." Formal word for *hirugohan.*

昼 This kanji means "noon." It shows the sun 日 rising high enough in the sky at noon to shine in the doorway (户) pictured on top, which is a separate radical created by borrowing only the left half of the "gate" radical 門 and distorting it a bit.

食 This kanji means "to eat." It shows a hand on top reaching in to a rice bowl in the middle and scooping up the rice with a spoon, pictured on the bottom.

daijoobu 大丈夫 / だいじょうぶ O.K.; all right; fine

*"****Die, Job****!" is what Satan wanted, but God made sure Job was O.K. in the end.*

Literally "big-strong-fellow." When a woman has a big, strong fellow to protect her, she should be *all right*. (Hey, fellow feminists, just looking for a mnemonic device here!) It may be amusing for you to know that 丈夫 means "husband" in Chinese.

大 This kanji means "big." It shows a person with his arms outstretched. "How big was that fish that got away?!"

丈 This character means "man." It shows a man striding forward confidently.

夫　This character also means "man," and like the character 丈 implies manliness. 夫 portrays a man who, to all appearances, has two sets of arms, emphasizing strength and robustness.

danna　だんな　husband

*Donna's husband, **Danna**, is a fine man. He goes by "**Dan**."*

Danna is used as an honorific if *-san* is added.

dare　誰 / だれ　who?

*Who would **dare** question their Japanese teacher's knowledge of the language?*

誰　The kanji has the "speech" radical 訁 on the left, since asking "who?" is something we say. The phonetic on the right is the "short-tailed bird" radical 隹; this is a common phonetic in many Chinese characters but does not work as such in Japanese for this word. Instead think of a short-tailed owl, whose hoot sounds like it's calling "who, who?"

denwa　電話 / でんわ　telephone

*When telemarketers call you on the telephone, a Scandinavian-American might say "**Den what** is it you want?!"*

Literally: "electric talk."

電　This kanji contains the "rain" radical 雨 on top, under which is a cloud with a tail of lightning coming out of it. The original meaning of the kanji was "lightning," from which people derived the idea of electricity. The kanji is now used as a common prefix for "electric." The simplified version shows the cloud with the tail of lightning, looking a bit like Ben Franklin's kite being struck by lightning.

話 This kanji, meaning "talk" or "speech," has the "speech" radical 言 on the left, showing a mouth (口) on the bottom with what appear to be sound waves coming above it, but what is actually breath rising. On the right of the kanji is a picture of a tongue protruding from a mouth (舌). The tongue serves as a phonetic that contributes to the meaning of the kanji as a whole, since speaking involves use of the tongue.

donata どなた who?

Who's got the ***donuts****?*

Formal for *dare.*

doo itashimashite どういたしまして "you're welcome"

*When the Japanese say "you're welcome" or "don't mention it," it sounds like they're saying "****don't touch my mustache****." It's nice that you're grateful, but touching my mustache is going too far!*

doobutsu 動物 / どうぶつ animal(s)

When you're around animals like deer, it's best to wear your ***doe boots****!*

Literally: "moving-thing."

動 This kanji means "to move." It has the "energy" radical 力 on the right, with the kanji 重 for "heavy" on the left as the phonetic. 重 seems to show weights piled up, as they would be at a gym. The metaphor in the kanji 動 is to use a lot of energy to move something heavy.

物 This kanji means "thing." It has the "cow" radical 牛 on the left, with the kanji 勿 on the right as the phonetic. 勿 means "to stop" and shows a banner that in ancient warfare was held up before the troops to order them to halt. However, 勿 looks like a hand milking the cow (牛).

In combination the two kanji 動物 literally mean "moving/animate things," i.e., animals.

doroboo どろぼう thief

*Thieves **do rob** us, if we're not careful.*

eigo 英語 / えいご English language

*Many Japanese language teachers insist that their students use no English in their classrooms. They want you to "**leggo** my eigo." However, the **ego** of some students makes them reluctant to **leggo** of their eigo.*

Literally: "English-language."

英 This kanji originally meant a type of flower. It has the "grass/flower" radical 艹 on top. The phonetic below shows a rectangle encircling the middle of a person (大) and means "center." It was used by the Chinese in the 19th century to transliterate the first syllable in "England." To remember this kanji, think about how well flowers grow in the mild, rainy climate of England, as an English gardener stands there proudly under his flowery trellis.

語 This kanji means "language." It is never used by itself, but is the suffix added to the names of the countries of the world to mean the language of that particular country. It has the "speech" radical 言 on the left. The phonetic 吾 on the right side was used for the pronoun "I" in classical Chinese. It has the "mouth" radical 口 on the bottom and the kanji for "five" 五 as the phonetic on top.

eki 駅 / えき train/subway station

*If you have to stand on a station platform for a long time in the cold, you'll start to feel very **achy**.*

駅 The kanji has the "horse" radical on the left, since in ancient times the stations were not for trains but for horse-drawn carriages. The phonetic on the right looks like a person leaning on a cane, waiting at the station for the carriage to arrive.

fun 分 / ふん minute

*You can have a lot of **fun** in a minute!*

分 This kanji as a verb means "to divide," but as a noun it means a small division of time, i.e., a minute. It shows a knife (刀) dividing something up by cutting it into two pieces (八).

furui 古い / ふるい old

*When our car gets old and breaks down, we say "**phooey**!" Or words to that effect.*

Used for things, not people.

古 The kanji is a composed of the kanji for "ten" 十 above the kanji for "mouth" 口. The *Shuowen Jiezi,* written nearly two millennia ago, explains that when something is passed down by word of mouth through ten generations, it is very old. The number "ten" is used metaphorically to mean a large number.

futoi ふとい thick; fat

*A **futon** is really thick, which makes it comfortable to sleep on.*

太 The kanji adds an extra stroke to the kanji for "big" 大 to create the kanji for thick, since when you have something that's already large and add to it, you make it even thicker.

futsuu 普通 / ふつう common; usual; ordinary

*It's common for human beings to walk around on two **foots**, unlike animals, which get around faster on four **foots**. [Sometimes you have to sacrifice grammar in the interest of a mnemonic device!]*

Literally: "general-pass through."

普 This kanji means "general; common." It has the "sun" 日 on the bottom. Certainly there is nothing new under the sun. The top part of the kanji is a symmetrical kanji 並 that shows two people lining up, as soldiers will do. Both the figures on the left and right are identical, contributing to the idea of "common; ordinary."

通 This kanji means "to pass through." It has the "walk" radical 辶 on the left. The phonetic on the right might be thought of fancifully as a person wearing a plaid shirt, which is common enough in the U.S., although not in Japan.

fuufu 夫婦 / ふうふ husband and wife

*When a husband and wife go out for a fancy dinner, they may put on some **foo foo** (cologne).*

Literally: "husband-wife."

夫 This kanji for "husband" shows a man with arms outstretched, displaying his strength.

婦 This kanji for "wife" has the "woman" radical 女 on the left. The right side shows a hand on top holding a cloth duster (巾) under the roof of the home, doing her wifely duties. Remember that old Chinese men made up these kanji two to three millennia ago.

gakkoo 学校 / がっこう school

*The Geico **gecko** obviously studied business in school, or he wouldn't know so much about car insurance.*

Literally: "learning-building."

学 This kanji means "study; learn." It's a simplification used in Japan and China after WWII of the original kanji 學 still used in Taiwan and Hong Kong and by Chinese in the West. The top part of the original kanji shows two hands on either side of two Xs, which represent what is being taught, and passing the knowledge to the student below, who is like a child (子) in his or her ignorance. The roof over the child's head symbolizes the confines of the student's mind. The purpose of study is to hopefully remove the roof, i.e., the barrier to learning, and allow true knowledge to enter. The simplified version reduces the entire top half of the character to three simple strokes, which you can think of as strings of knowledge entering the student's mind.

geri 下痢 / げり diarrhea

*When the steel mills of **Gary**, Indiana still belched out tons of polluting smoke into the air, I would imagine many inhabitants of **Gary** experienced bouts of diarrhea, among other ailments.*

Literally: "downward-drip."

下 This kanji means "down; falling." Here it describes the falling of waste from one's rear when suffering diarrhea. The vertical and slanted lines in the kanji point downward from the horizontal stroke on top, which represents the ground.

痢 This kanji means "drip." The left and top parts of the kanji are the "sickness" radical 疒, which shows the body as a structure around us, with a roof and sidewall. The two little skewed lines on the far left show germs assailing the body. Some of my students describe the "sickness" radical as a bed, with the two feet of the patient sticking out on the far left and a hot water bottle on the very top. The phonetic for 痢 is 利, which by itself means "benefit" or "advantage." It is composed of two radicals, namely the "grain" radical on the left and the "sword" radical on the right. The actual etymology is that when you cut down the grain with a sharp instrument like a scythe, you reap the benefits. In the context of diarrhea, think of the body releasing the waste from eating grain, with the knife symbolizing the pain of this condition.

ha 歯 / は tooth

*When a dentist asks a patient to open wide to look at a troublesome tooth, the Japanese may say "**ha**" (tooth!) while we Americans say "**ah**."*

歯 The kanji used in Japan after WWII is a simplification of the traditional kanji 齒 still used in Taiwan and Hong Kong and by Chinese in the West. Below the phonetic, which is the foot at rest (止), is a depiction of two rows of teeth. The simplified kanji used in modern Japanese substitutes the kanji for "rice" 米 for the two rows of teeth—appropriate enough, since it is often rice that gets stuck in the teeth of Japanese people when they eat.

haha 母 / はは my mother [humble]

*Quit that "**ha, ha**"! My mother is no laughing matter!*

母 The kanji shows a mother's two breasts, turned 90 degrees to make it easier to write. The breasts refer to a mother nursing an infant.

hajime 初め / はじめ beginning

*"**Ha, Jimmy**, this is only the beginning!" is what Jimmy Stewart's agent must have said to him after his first movie was a hit.*

初 The kanji has the "clothes" radical 衤 on the left and the "sword" radical 刀 on the right. When you begin to make clothing, you must first cut the cloth, explained the 2nd-century Chinese etymological text *Shuowen Jiezi*.

hajimeru 始める / はじめる (to) begin

The annual pilgrimage made by Muslims to Mecca, called the ***Hajj, may*** *begin on various dates depending on the year, since it's based on the lunar calendar.*

Hajimeru is the transitive form; *hajimaru* is intransitive.

始 The kanji has the "woman" radical 女 on the left, symbolizing that life begins for all of us in the womb of a woman, namely our mothers. The right side shows a nose on top of a mouth. When we're in the embryonic stage we're only a little nose and mouth, etc.

hakken 発見 / はっけん discovery

*When Barbie made the discovery they had created a boyfriend for her, she must have exclaimed "****Ha, Ken****!"*

Literally: "send forth-see."

発 This kanji is one of the most common prefixes for verbs that are kanji compounds. It has the meaning of "to send out; emit." It looks like a crossbow on the bottom (开), shooting out arrows at the top. This is a modern simplification of the original kanji 發, still used in Taiwan and Hong Kong and by Chinese in the West. It shows two hands on the bottom right, holding out a bow on the bottom left, with the top part symbolizing a hunter striding forward to shoot some prey.

見 This kanji means "to see" and simply shows an eye (目) on two legs.

hanashimasu 話します / はなします speak

Hannah [Montana], she *must speak to the press all the time.*

話 The kanji has the "speech" radical 言 on the left, showing breath rising up from a mouth (口). The phonetic 舌 on the right is the kanji for "tongue." It shows the tongue sticking out of the mouth. When the Japanese speak and you haven't studied the language, they seem to be speaking "in tongues." In any case, like all of us, they are speaking with their tongues.

hantai 反対 / はんたい oppose

*Should your boss oppose your idea, you are **hand-tied**, i.e., your hands are tied.*

Literally: "upside down-facing." Often used with *suru*.

反 This kanji means "upside down" or "turned over." It shows a hand (又) being turned over (厂).

対 This kanji means "to face" someone or something. The original pictograph 對, still used in Taiwan and Hong Kong and by Chinese in the West, shows a hand on the right (寸) facing a thicket of dense vegetation. After World War II, when some kanji were simplified to promote literacy, the thicket on the left was changed to what appears to be a hand (又) opposing the hand on the right. In mainland China it's now written as 对, but the Japanese add an extra stroke on the top of the hand on the left.

harau 払う / はらう pay

*When you owe creditors money, they often **harass** you until you pay.*

払 The kanji has the "hand" radical 扌 on the left, with the outline of a nose on the right. When you pay college tuition or for a new car, it feels like we're paying through the nose as we hand over the money!

haru 春 / はる spring

*"Spring is **haru** (**here**)!" exclaim people in northern climes, when the weather starts to turn warm after a long, cold winter.*

春 The kanji shows plants coming out of the ground in the spring under the influence of the sun's warmth, according to the Chinese etymological text *Shuowen Jiezi.*

hataraku 働く / はたらく work

*If you really intend to work hard, you must hang your **hat** on a **rack** and get down to it.*

働 The kanji has the "person" radical 亻 on the left, since it is people who have to work a job, as opposed to animals. The phonetic on the right is the kanji 動, which means "to move." 動 has the "energy" radical 力 on the right, since movement requires some amount of energy. Its phonetic on the left, 重, means "heavy," and shows weights piled up. The phonetic contributes to the meaning, referring to moving something heavy. Work often involves moving heavy objects, especially for the vast majority of people in ancient China.

hen 変 / へん strange

*The **hen** is a very strange animal to us humans, as we watch them strut around the barnyard.*

変 The kanji by itself means "change." When things change, we often find the new reality strange. The radical on the bottom shows two hands, in this case acting to change something. The top part looks like a person standing straight with arms held defiantly to either side, determined to change something. This top part is actually a simplification after WWII in both Japan and mainland China of what was really a phonetic in the traditional kanji, 變. This has the "speech" radical 言 in between two silkworm cocoons. Perhaps this phonetic was even intended to contribute to the meaning, since silkworms undergo an amazing change from caterpillar to chrysalis to moth, and because people's words are often so changeable.

heta 下手 / へた bad/poor at something

*When you are poor at something, you tend to **hate** it.*

Literally: "lower/inferior-hand."

下 This kanji means "below; underneath" and here implies "lower" or "inferior" in ability. The vertical and slanted lines point downward from the horizontal stroke on top, which represents the ground.

手 This kanji means "hand." The three horizontal lines represent three of the fingers on a hand, with the vertical line representing the wrist.

heya 部屋 / へや room

*When someone unexpectedly walks into your room, you might say "**Hey**, what are you doing in my room?!"*

Literally: "section of a house."

部 This kanji means "part; section." It has the "city wall" radical on the right, which shows the outline of the building blocks of a city wall. The phonetic on the left is a distortion of the "speech" radical 言. A lot of talking goes on in rooms, after all.

屋 This kanji means "house." Although it is written with the "corpse" radical 尸, it should be thought of as the "doorway" radical 戸 since the top stroke was accidentally omitted when the kanji was codified several millennia ago. Beneath the doorway is a bird nosediving down to the ground (土).

hikimasu 弾きます / ひきます play a string instrument

*When you play the violin or viola, you end up with a **hickey** on your neck!*

弾 The kanji shows an archer's bow on the left (弓), which depends on a taut bowstring to shoot its arrows. It is used to mean playing an instrument with strings, including the violin, viola, cello, and bass, as well as the piano, harp, and guitar. The phonetic 単 on the right by itself means "single." After WWII it was slightly simplified from its original form, 單, which shows two mouths on top and a pitchfork on the bottom. It was meant to show assailing an enemy in single-hand combat with loud cries and a pitchfork, which was the nature of war in ancient times.

hikooki 飛行機 / ひこうき airplane

*At the beginning of the 1900s, when a pilot would first go up in one of the early airplanes, people would point to him and exclaim "**he's kooky**!"*

Literally: "flying-going-machine."

飛 The kanji looks like a bird ascending to the sky (廾) on its two wings (飞). While the kanji actually does contain the pictograph for wing doubled, combined with the kanji 升 that means "to ascend," the original pictograph actually portrayed the mythical phoenix in flight.

行 The kanji seems to show an intersection of two roads. It actually depicts footprints. Hence the meaning of "to go."

機 This kanji meaning "machine" has the "tree" radical on the left, indicating that the earliest machines in China were made of wood. The phonetic on the right side, often found in kanji and pronounced *ki* in the onyomi, means "several." It shows two silkworm cocoons on top (丝) and two halberds on the bottom (戈). A machine that could produce bolts of silk as well as weapons would be a remarkable machine, indeed!

hima 暇 / ひま free time

***Hima** got free time, but I don't.*

暇　The kanji has the "sun" radical on the left, found in many kanji related to time, since before watches and clocks humans relied on the sun to tell the time of day. The phonetic on the right of the kanji looks like a person standing on the left and facing right toward a table on which is placed some drink they're enjoying in their free time.

hoka 他 / ほか another

*Rather than stick two coats on one hook, you can always put the second coat on another **hook**.*

他　The kanji has the "person" radical 亻 on the left, since the original idea was any person other than the ones included in the conversation. The right side of the kanji is the word for "also" in Chinese. It's presumed by etymologists to be the outline of a jar or pot, and was used because that word was a homophone with the word for "also." The combination of the "person" radical with the kanji for "other" was intended to mean "and also that other person or people not here with us." It came to mean simply "other."

homeru ほめる praise

*The ancient Greek poet, **Homer**, praises his hero, Odysseus, in his epic poem* The Odyssey.

hoomen 方面 / ほうめん direction

Homing *pigeons have an amazing ability to head in the direction of **home**.*

Literally: "place-surface."

方　This kanji means "place." It looks like a square boat lashed to the shore. Since the boat is tied to the shore at a certain location, it came to mean "place." According to the 2nd-century Chinese etymological text *Shuowen Jiezi*, it may well be a deliberate distortion of the Buddhist "swastika" 卍, which symbolizes that God is everywhere and in every place, north, south, east, west, above, and below.

面　This kanji means "mask," which is what it depicts. However, in kanji compounds it has come to mean "surface; side," referring to which side something is facing.

hon　本 / ほん　book(s)

*We read books to **hone** our knowledge of a subject.*

本　The small horizontal line at the bottom of the "tree" radical 木 emphasizes the root of the tree. The actual etymology is that books are the root or origin of learning.

hoohoo　方法 / ほうほう　method; way

*Santa Claus, with his "**ho, ho, ho**," has a special method for delivering all those presents around the world at Christmas.*

Literally: "square-way."

方　This kanji means "square." It looks like a square boat lashed to the shore. Since a boat is tied to the shore at a certain location, the kanji also came to mean "place." According to the 2nd-century Chinese etymological text *Shuowen Jiezi*, the kanji may well be a deliberate distortion of the Buddhist "swastika" 卍, basically square in shape, which symbolizes that God is everywhere and in every place, north, south, east, west, above, and below.

hoshi　星 / ほし　star

*When I wish on a star, I think, "**Hope she** will come to love me."*

星　The kanji on the top has the star that is our sun as the radical. The phonetic 生 on the bottom shows a plant coming out of the ground bearing a fruit or blossom and means "to give birth to." The stars give birth to the planets, after all.

hoshii 欲しい / ほしい want; desire (something)

Ho, she *really wants a diamond ring!*

欲 The radical on the right side of the kanji shows a person on the bottom, with breath rising up. When we really desire something, we tend to breathe heavily. The phonetic in this kanji is on the left side. The two sets of slanted lines at the top indicate the folds of a mountain valley, with the small box on the bottom not a mouth but rather the valley itself. However, it looks a bit like a gentleman with slanted eyes and a mustache, with his mouth open in desire.

ikimasu 行きます / いきます go

When you try to go anywhere in winter in the north of the U.S. or Japan, the roads are an ***icky mess****!*

行 The kanji seems to show an intersection of two roads. It actually depicts footprints. Hence the meaning of to go.

imooto 妹 / いもうと younger sister [humble]

My little sister is very emotional and ***emotes*** *a lot.*

妹 As in almost all the kanji for female relatives, the radical is the "woman" radical 女. The phonetic 未 on the right shows a tree on which the top branches haven't yet grown out. Younger sisters are like trees that haven't fully developed.

isha 医者 / いしゃ doctor

When my doctor gives me a ***shot****, "****ee!****" is what I say!*

Literally: "medicine-person."

医 This kanji means "medicine." It depicts an arrow (矢) being removed from a wound in the body, represented by the three sides of the box surrounding the arrow. This is a simplification of the original kanji 醫 still used by the Chinese in Taiwan and Hong Kong and in the West, which on the top right shows a hand holding a scalpel and removing an arrow from a wound on the top left, then disinfecting the wound with alcohol (酒), shown on the bottom but minus the "water" radical 氵. Since the element 医 only appeared in 醫, after WWII the kanji was simplified as 医 in both Japan and mainland China.

者 This kanji is often used as a suffix for various professions, in which case it means "person." It's the *sha* in *geisha* (芸者), for example. The top part shows the head of a person, and not the "earth" radical. Whenever 土 appears at the top of a kanji, rather than on the left side, it generally represents a person's head. What appears to be the sun at the bottom of the kanji 者 actually represents a mouth filled with talk. Hence the idea that a person who practices a certain profession has a lot to say on the subject of his or her expertise.

isu 椅 / いす chair

No other chair is quite as comfortable as an ***EZ*** *Boy recliner.*

椅 This kanji means "chair." It has the "tree" radical on the left, since furniture in ancient times was always made of wood. The phonetic on the right means "strange; odd." It shows a person on top with their arms stretched out (大). The bottom part shows breath emanating from the mouth (可), calling out in surprise at seeing something strange. But what it looks like is a person sitting on a stool, with an ashtray on the bottom right.

子 This kanji, which shows a child in swaddling clothes, is a common suffix for nouns in Chinese and does not contribute to the meaning. Although it certainly is lovely to have your child on your lap when you sit in a chair.

itadakimasu 頂きます / いただきます I (humbly) receive

The Japanese one word prayer before every meal, itadakimasu, sounds a bit like ***eat a dirty mouse****!*

頂 The kanji originally meant the top of the head. It has the "head" radical 頁 on the right, with the kanji for "nail" or "tack" 丁 on the left as the phonetic. When we pray before a meal, we bow our heads, showing the crown of the head. It seems an apt metaphor for humbly receiving a meal.

itai 痛い / いたい painful

Some boys find wearing a ***tie*** *painful, especially if their Mom* ***ties*** *it too tightly. "****Ee, tie****! It hurts!" the boys might say.*

痛 The kanji has the "sickness" radical 疒 on the left, which shows the body as a structure around us, with a roof and side-wall. The two little skewed lines on the far left show germs assailing the body. Some of my students describe the "sickness" radical as a bed, with the two feet of the patient sticking out on the far left and a hot water bottle on the very top. The phonetic 甬 on the right might be thought of fancifully as a person whose head has a tight collar around it and whose arms and legs below are bound by ropes or chains, and therefore is in pain.

itsu いつ when?

When ***it's*** *an* ***itch****, try not to scratch.*

jidai 時代 / じだい era; age; period of time

*Studying history as a child, I exclaimed "****gee****, in every age of human history people would* ***die*** *from war."*

Literally: "time-generation."

時 This kanji means "time." It has the "sun" radical 日 on the left, since before cellphones and watches people depended on the sun to know the time of day. The phonetic 寺 on the right means "Buddhist temple." The striking of the bells in the temples at certain times of day announces the hours of prayer. 寺 does look a bit like a hand on the bottom with a wrist watch on the top.

代 This kanji means "generation." It has the "person" radical 亻 on the left and the "dart" radical on the right. Human beings unfortunately continue to use weapons against one another in generation after generation.

jisho 辞書 / じしょ dictionary

*If we would speak to our dictionary, we would say "**gee, show** me what this word means."*

Literally: "word-book."

辞 This kanji means "word." It has the "tongue" radical on the left, which depicts the tongue sticking out from the mouth (口). The phonetic on the right side means "hard" in the sense of painful. It actually shows a prisoner in manacles and chains. The top two strokes are the head and neck; the two short slanted lines are the hands in manacles; the bottom two horizontal lines depict chains on the legs; and the vertical stroke is the torso of the prisoner. When we don't know what a word means, it shackles our understanding.

書 This kanji means "book." It shows a hand on the top holding a writing brush represented by the vertical line, with the bristles pressed down flat on the paper, writing down something that you want to say. Those words are represented by the mouth on the bottom of the character, with the horizontal line in the box representing the mouth filled with speech (曰).

jitensha 自転車 / じてんしゃ bicycle

*Bicycles now have as many as 20 or 30 gears. But back when bikes only had 3 gears and the 10-speed bike came out, people like me exclaimed "**gee, ten** speeds!"*

Literally: "self-propelling vehicle."

自 This kanji shows the nose in profile. Chinese and Japanese people will point to their nose rather than their chest, when they emphasize they're talking about themselves. The pictograph for nose came to represent "self."

転 This kanji has the "cart" radical on the left, appropriate for the sense of driving or propelling a wheeled vehicle forward. The right side, a simplification of the original phonetic, has the kanji for "two" above a simple pictograph of the nose in profile. Two people nose (know) better than one how to propel a car out of snow or mud!

車 The character actually shows a cart, with the top and bottom horizontal strokes representing the wheels, the long vertical stroke showing the axle, and the middle section portraying the body of the cart, all from a bird's-eye view.

jiyuu 自由 / じゆう freedom; free

*When people from more repressive countries emigrate to the U.S., they likely are thinking, "**Gee, you** are really free here!"*

Literally: "self-from."

自 This kanji shows the nose in profile and represents "self," since Chinese and Japanese will point to their nose rather than their chest to emphasize they are talking about themselves.

由 This kanji shows a rice field (田), with the center vertical line indicating something or someone coming out from the field.

Freedom is the ability to have your actions come out of your own decisions.

joozu 上手 / じょうず good at something; skillful

***Joe's** good at jazz. And **Joe's zoo** is very skillful when it comes to handling dangerous animals.*

Literally: "upper/superior-hand."

上 This kanji means "above; on top of" and in this context implies "superior." The vertical line and small horizontal line on top depict upward motion from the ground, which is represented by the bottom horizontal stroke.

手 This kanji means "hand." The three horizontal lines represent three of the fingers on a hand, with the vertical line representing the wrist.

josei 女性 / じょせい woman; female

*Josephine, or **Josie** as I call her, is a lovely woman.*

Literally: "female-gender."

女 This kanji means "female." It shows a woman with her arms and legs crossed, bowing submissively. Clearly this is a kanji devised by Chinese men three millennia ago, and indicative of the position of Chinese and Japanese women until the past century.

性 This kanji means "gender," as well as "temperament; nature." It has the "heart" radical 忄 on the left. The phonetic 生 on the right is the kanji meaning "to give birth" and is the *sei* in 先生 (*sensei,* "teacher") and 学生 (*gakusei,* "student"). It shows a plant coming out of the ground bearing a fruit or a blossom. When we are born, our gender and temperament are determined, or at least so the kanji seems to argue.

junbi 準備 / じゅんび preparation

A preparation of something ***jumbo*** *sometimes turns out to be a real* ***jumble****.*

Literally: "definite-preparation." Often used with *suru*.

準 This kanji in Chinese means "exactly; precisely," but in Japanese has come to mean "quasi-" or "semi-." It has the character 十 on the bottom as the radical, indicating that something that's been done is a perfect "10." The phonetic on the top has the "water" radical 氵 on the left and the "short-tailed bird" radical 隹 on the right. When a bird dives down from the sky into the water, it has to take definite aim. The true etymology is about a hunter needing to shoot very definitely, i.e., precisely, in order to bring down a bird.

備 This kanji means "prepare." It has the "person" radical 亻 on the left, for it is people who make preparations for various things, such as preparing the fields for cultivation. The right side of the kanji has the "grass/flower" radical 艹 on the top, found in the kanji for various flowers, vegetables, and herbs, as well as tea. Below that is a roof with a side wall, under which is the character "to use" 用, showing a hand holding a tool that a person wishes to use. A useful mnemonic might be to think about a man preparing to propose to a woman under the roof by using flowers to enhance the mood.

kaban かばん bag; book bag; backpack

Be careful to not leave your bag or backpack in the ***cabin*** *of a boat or in a* ***cab on*** *the seat!*

kado 角 / かど corner

Only a ***cad*** *stands on the corner ogling the women who pass by.*

角　The kanji shows the horn of a bull, with the crossed lines representing the striations on the horn. The corner of a street has sharp angles, like the horn of a bull.

kaisha　会社 / かいしゃ　company

*Every company is concerned with making lots of **cash**.*

Literally: "gathering-society."

会　This kanji means "meeting; gathering." Under a roof is the character for "two" above the outline of a nose. It seems to be showing two noses, representing two people, meeting under a roof. After all, two nose (knows) better than one! The truth is that this kanji is a simplification used in both China and Japan after WWII of the kanji 會, still used in Hong Kong and Taiwan and among Chinese Americans, which shows two people talking in a doorway under a roof. The 日 on the bottom represents a mouth filled with talk, rather than the sun.

社　This kanji means "society." It has the "god" radical 礻 on the left, with the kanji for "earth" on the right. The true etymology is that it represents the emperor praying to God every year for a good harvest on behalf of the entire society.

kakimasu　書きます / かきます　write

*When we write something we must not get too **cocky** and forget to first check the facts we claim to be reporting.*

書　The kanji shows a hand on the top holding a writing brush represented by the vertical line, with the bristles pressed down flat on the paper, writing down something that you want to say. Those words are represented by the mouth on the bottom of the character, with the horizontal line in the box representing the mouth filled with speech (日).

kami 神 / かみ god; god(s)

A ***Commie*** *doesn't believe in God.*

神 The kanji has the "god" radical ネ on the left. When this radical appears on the left of a kanji, it looks a bit like a man in a necktie, turning to the right and heading to church. In reality it's a deliberate distortion of an altar (示) on which something (一) is placed on top as an offering to God. The phonetic on the right side of 神 has a vertical line extending out from a farmer's field (田) and means "to extend." God extends his bounty to us, including the bounty of the fields.

kanai 家内 / かない my wife [humble]

Can I *tell you stories about my wife! I can, but I won't!*

Literally: "home-inside."

家 This kanji means "home" and shows a pig under a roof. The pig is turned 90 degrees to make it easier to write, with four legs on the left and the tail sticking out at the bottom right. The Chinese could never afford the wasteful practice of raising cows, which necessitates large tracts of land to graze, as their main source of meat. Peasant homes often had pigs sleeping with people under the same roof, albeit in a sty at the other end of the house from the family bedrooms.

内 This kanji shows a person within a room, conveying the idea of "within." The place for a woman in traditional China or Japan was in the home.

kanari かなり relatively; fairly

The ***canary*** *is a relatively small bird.*

kanojo 彼女 / かのじょ she; her

Can O.J. *really have killed her, his lovely wife?!*

Literally: "that-woman."

彼 This kanji means "he; his." It has the "step" 彳 radical on the left. Originally the kanji meant another person, as opposed to "you" or "I." The phonetic 皮 on the right side means "skin." It shows a hand 又 on the bottom right using a knife to scrape the hide off an animal.

女 This kanji means "female." It shows a woman with her arms and legs crossed, bowing submissively. Clearly it's a kanji devised by Chinese men three millennia ago, and indicative of the position of Chinese and Japanese women until the past century.

kantan 簡単 / かんたん simple

Doing the ***can-can*** *is anything but* *simple!*

Literally: "simple-single."

簡 This kanji means "simple." It has the "bamboo" radical ⺮ on the top. The original meaning of this kanji was a single, simple slip of bamboo on which a message was written. The phonetic 日 on the bottom shows the sun in the middle of a door or gate (門) and means "in between." Think about how simple it is to write a note on bamboo or paper when the sun is shining in our doorway and we can see clearly.

単 This kanji means "single." After WWII it was slightly simplified from its original form, 單, which shows two mouths on top and a pitchfork on the bottom. It was meant to show assailing an enemy in single-hand combat with loud cries and a pitchfork, which was the nature of war in ancient times.

kao 顔 / かお face

A ***cow*** *has particularly sweet face, with those big cow eyes.*

顔 The kanji has the "head" radical 頁 on the right. The left side shows the shading of the face.

karada 体 / からだ body

*When you get a **karate** chop to the body, it really hurts!*

体 The kanji has the "person" radical 亻 on the left, referring to the human body. The phonetic 本 on the right shows a tree with a small horizontal line drawn near the base to indicate the root of the tree. The body is the root or base of human beings. This kanji is actually a simplification used in Japan and China since WWII of the traditional kanji still used in Hong Kong and Taiwan and by Chinese in the West. The original kanji 體 has a very different radical and phonetic. It has the "bone" radical 骨 on the left, appropriate for a kanji for the body. The phonetic on the right shows two hands on top placing a ritual vessel (豆) on the altar of a temple, perhaps in prayer for bodily health.

karai 辛い / からい spicy; hot

*"**Ay, caramba**, that's hot!" you might say after eating a tamale with hot sauce.*

辛 The kanji originally meant "hard" in the sense of painful. It actually shows a prisoner in manacles and chains. The top two strokes are the head and neck; the two short slanted lines are the hands in manacles; the bottom two horizontal lines depict chains on the legs; and the vertical stroke is the torso of the prisoner. A hard fate, indeed! Since the kanji is now used in Japanese to mean "hot; spicy," think about it showing a person with arms outstretched exclaiming, "Ay, caramba, that's spicy!"

karappo 空っぽ / からっぽ empty

*When you find the refrigerator empty, you might say to yourself, "oh, **karappo**!"*

空 The kanji has the "cave" radical on top, consisting of a roof with eaves, with the two slanted lines below the roof showing the concavity of the cave. The phonetic 工 at the bottom shows a carpenter's rule for drawing straight lines, with the vertical line in the middle being the handle.

kare 彼 / かれ he; him

*That Nascar racer, he takes really good **care** of his **car**.*

彼 The kanji has the "step" radical on the left. Originally the kanji meant another person, as opposed to "you" or "I." It has come to mean "he" in Japanese. The phonetic 皮 on the right side means "skin." It shows a hand 又 on the bottom right using a knife to scrape the hide off an animal—definitely he-man work.

kariru 借りる / かりる borrow; rent

*It's fine to borrow money on occasion, but don't make a **career** out of it!*

借 The character has the "person" radical 亻 on the left. It is only people who lend or borrow things. Animals just take what they want without asking. The right side of the character appears to have a shorthand version of the number 21, written in Chinese as 二十一, on top, with the character 日 for "sun" or "day" on the bottom. 21 days is exactly the period of time that we can borrow books from the library.

kasa 傘 / かさ umbrella

*So many umbrellas look alike that we often find ourselves saying to others "Mi **kasa** or su **kasa**?"*

傘 This kanji actually depicts an umbrella. The two slanting lines on top show the protective top of the umbrella, with the long vertical line representing the handle. The four little 人 are not people but rather depict the spokes that support the top of the umbrella. Several decades ago the *Chicago Tribune*, in a Sunday column entitled "Learn a Chinese Character a Week," explained it as showing ten (十) people (人) who were required to make an umbrella on an assembly line. While this is bogus etymology, as a writer of a book on fanciful mnemonic devices I can hardly cast stones!

kashu 歌手 / かしゅ singer

A ***cashew*** *is a nut, and so is many a singer!*

Literally: "song-hand."

歌 This kanji shows two mouths on the left, with breath arising from them representing singing (可). The left side of this kanji, 哥, was the original kanji for "song." However, since in Chinese the word for "older brother" is pronounced exactly the same and is written as 哥, to avoid confusion the Chinese added a pictograph showing a person exhaling breath (欠).

手 This kanji means "hand." The three horizontal strokes represent some of the fingers of the hand, with the vertical line representing the wrist.

kasu 貸す / かす lend

'Cause *I care about you, I'll* lend *you the money.*

貸 The kanji has a cowry shell, the "shell" radical 貝, on the bottom. Cowry shells were used as currency in ancient China before the invention of copper coins and silver ingots, so it's appropriate to have this radical in the kanji "to lend," since it's often money that is lent. The phonetic on the top is the kanji 代, which means "generation." It has the "person" radical 亻 on the left and the "dart" radical 弋 on the right. Human beings unfortunately continue to use weapons against one another in generation after generation. To remember the kanji 貸, think about how people will lend you money, but often there's a hidden weapon held by the lender, that we call the "interest" on a loan.

The "-masu" form of *kasu* is *kashimasu*. Think about how banks lend cash to their customers.

kata 方 / かた person

*The jazz musician introduced me to his drummer by saying "this **cat** is the person who keeps the beat in our band."*

方 This kanji means "square" as well as "place." It looks like a square boat lashed to the shore. Since a boat is tied to the shore at a certain location, the kanji came to also mean "place." According to the 2nd-century Chinese etymological text *Shuowen Jiezi*, it may well be a deliberate distortion of the Buddhist "swastika" 卍, which symbolizes that God is everywhere and in every place, north, south, east, west, above, and below.

When used as a single kanji and not in combination with other kanji *kata* is the formal word for person.

katsu かつ win

***Cats** are winning out over dogs as the most numerous pet in American homes.*

The *-masu* form of *katsu* is *kachimasu*. Think about how in ballgames like baseball or football you have to catch the ball to win.

katsudoo 活動 / かつどう activities

***Cats do** engage in a lot of entertaining activities, which is why their videos are so popular on YouTube.*

Literally: "living-movements."

活 This kanji means "to live." It has the "water" radical 氵 on the left, since water is the most crucial requirement for life. The phonetic on the right adds to the meaning, since it shows the tongue (舌), which mammals use to lap up water.

動　This kanji means "to move." It has the "energy" radical 力 on the right, with the kanji for "heavy" 重 on the left as the phonetic and that seems to show weights piled up, as they would be at a gym. The suggestion is that we use a lot of energy to move something heavy.

kau 買う / かう　buy

*To buy a **cow** in previous centuries was a really major purchase for a peasant.*

買　The kanji actually shows a net on the top, with a cowry shell, the "money" radical, on the bottom. In ancient China, cowry shells were used as currency. When you went to buy something, you would scoop up a bunch of cowry shells to go make a purchase.

kaze 風邪 / かぜ　cold (the virus)

***'Cause** of the common cold, millions of us have to miss work every year.*

Literally: "wind-wickedness."

風　This kanji means "wind." It has the "insect" radical 虫 under a single slanted line, indicating that the insects are hiding. The strokes that surround the insect on the two sides and the very top indicate the blowing of the wind. The 2nd-century Chinese etymological text *Shuowen Jiezi* explains that "when the wind blows, the insects breed." I prefer to remember it by thinking that when the wind blows, the insects hide and don't bother you when you're enjoying a picnic.

邪　This kanji means "evil; wicked." It has the "city wall" radical on the right, which outlines the building blocks of a city wall. The left side is the kanji 牙 for "tooth," which is the outline of a sharp canine tooth. Not knowing the etymology of the kanji 邪, I remember it by picturing the right side as the head and big belly of my dentist, extracting a tooth. He means well by me, but it sure seems evil at the time!

kega けが injury

*When the fraternity boys drunkenly moved more **kegs** of beer into their fraternity house, they suffered an injury.*

keiken 経験 / けいけん experience

*Getting **cake on** your birthday is a delightful, if fattening, experience.*

Literally: "pass through-examine."

経 This kanji means "pass through." It has the "thread" radical 糸 on the left, referring to silk having to pass through an arduous process of raising silkworms, boiling the cocoons they eventually make, and unravelling the thin filaments to create silk threads. The phonetic on the right was simplified after WWII to show a hand (又) on top with the "earth" radical 土 on the bottom. The experience of most people in ancient China or Japan was to get their hands dirty by working the soil.

験 This kanji means "examine; test." It has the "horse" radical 馬 on the left, since before buying a horse the buyer would always carefully examine it. The phonetic on the right of 験 was simplified after WWII. It now seems to show a person (大) under a shelter, perhaps examining the horse to determine its condition.

kekka 結果 / けっか result

*The result of every birthday party is a **cake**.*

Literally: "tie together-fruits."

結 This kanji, which means "to tie," has the "thread" radical 糸 on the left, indicating silk thread. The phonetic on the right means "good luck." The "mouth" radical 口 on the bottom is that of a fortune teller with arms akimbo (士). Hopefully the soothsayer is saying that the odds are 10 (十) to 1 (一) that the results of some action will be fortuitous. This kanji is also used in the kanji compound for "marriage," 結婚 (*kekkon*), which uses the metaphor of "tying" a couple together through the bonds of marriage. The same basic metaphor of "tying together" is employed in the kanji compound here for "result," which is the consequence that is tied to the actions that preceded it.

果 This kanji means "fruit." It is the same metaphor that we use in English when we talk about the "fruits" of one's labor, although in English that always refers to a positive result, while in Japanese it is not necessarily a good or bad result. The kanji 果 shows a tree bearing a fruit on top, which the ancient scribes made to look exactly like the "field" radical.

kekkon 結婚 / けっこん marriage

A marriage custom is to have ***cake on*** *your wedding day.*

Literally: "tie the knot of marriage."

結 This kanji, which means "to tie," has the "thread" radical 糸 on the left, indicating silk thread. The phonetic on the right means "good luck." The "mouth" radical 口 on the bottom is that of a fortune teller with arms akimbo (士). Hopefully the soothsayer is saying that the odds are 10 (十) to 1 (一) that the couple will have good fortune.

婚 This kanji means "marriage." It has the "woman" radical 女 on the left. Since Chinese men created this written language two to three millennia ago, they thought of marriage in terms of a man taking a bride. The phonetic on the right, which means "dusk," shows the sun on the bottom (日) and a water plant stretching out its tendrils below the surface of the water (氏). When a man marries, it is the sun setting on his bachelor years.

kekkoo けっこう fine; just right

***Cake? Oh**, that's just fine!*

Often used with *desu*.

kenka けんか quarrel

*Ken started to quarrel with Barbie over the fact that there is a Barbie car but no **Ken car**.*

Often used with *desu*.

kinjo 近所 / きんじょ neighborhood

*Joe is very **keen** on his neighborhood.*

Literally: "near-place."

近 This kanji means "near; close." It has the "walk" radical ⻌ on the left. The phonetic on the right, an axe, contributes to the meaning. It refers to ancient combat, in which the warrior had to get close enough to his enemy to hew him with an axe.

所 This kanji means "place." It is composed of two radicals: the "doorway" radical 戸 on the left and the "axe" radical 斤 on the right. When building a home for yourself in ancient times, you wielded an axe to cut a doorway.

kinoo 昨日 / きのう yesterday

*John Lennon of the Beatles was very **keen on** yesterday.*

Literally: "yesterday-day."

昨 This kanji by itself means "yesterday." The kanji for "day" 日 is really redundant. 昨 has the "sun" radical on the left, which is the radical in many characters related to time. The phonetic on the right depicts the hand of a person, perhaps counting on the fingers the various things that happened yesterday.

kippu 切符 / きっぷ ticket

*Be sure to **keep** your ticket when you get on the train, since you'll need it to feed it into the machine at the turnstile when you arrive at your destination.*

Literally: "cut-tally."

切 This kanji means "to cut." It has the "knife" 刀 radical on the right with the kanji 七 for "seven" on the left as the phonetic. Think of cutting things into seven or more pieces. The ticket is a piece of paper cut down to a small size.

符 This kanji means a "tally" or "marker." It has the "bamboo" radical ⺮ on the top, since in ancient China markers for counting were made of bamboo. The phonetic on the bottom has the "person" radical 亻 on the left and a hand extended on the right, which means "to pay." People extend their hand to show their ticket when entering the theater.

kirai 嫌い / きらい dislike

*I dislike **rye** whiskey!*

嫌 The Chinese men of several millennia ago felt that women were more apt than men to be picky and to express their distaste for something, hence the "woman" radical 女 on the left. The phonetic on the right seems to show a bundle of firewood, tied together at the top. Any woman would dislike having to carry a heavy load like that!

kirei きれい pretty; clean

Many people have pretty ***key rings****.*

kissaten 喫茶店 / きっさてん coffee house

Coffee houses are very romantic places, where couples can go to enjoy coffee and ***kiss at ten*** *a.m. when they open.*

Literally: "eat-tea-shop."

喫 This kanji means "eat." It has the "mouth" radical 口 on the left, appropriately enough. The complex phonetic on the right shows a plant on the top left, a knife on the top right (刀), and a person with arms outstretched on the bottom. Think about a chef cutting up vegetables to cook and eat.

茶 This kanji for "tea" has the "grass/flower" radical 艹 found at the top of characters for flowers, vegetables, and herbs. Below the "grass/flower" radical is a shelter under which a large tea plant, represented by the "tree" radical 木, is being dried, before the leaves are plucked off to make tea.

店 This kanji means "store." It shows the roof and side wall of a store (广). The phonetic under the roof, shows the mouth of a fortune teller on the bottom who can read the cracks in a tortoise shell to foretell the future (占). However, 占 looks a bit like a sign pointing to women's blouses or men's slacks in the store.

Note: When coffee houses sprang up in Japan in the 20th century, the closest equivalent in the Japanese experience was the teahouses, which served both tea and snacks. Hence the Japanese term for coffee houses, namely, "eating tea shops." The Cantonese in southeastern China still talk about "eating tea" when enjoying tea and snack foods in "dim sum" restaurants.

kitanai 汚い / きたない dirty

Keep an eye *on the floor, to make sure you vacuum it before it gets too dirty.*

汚 The kanji has the "water" radical 氵 on the left, since we generally clean things with water. Think of the phonetic on the right side as either layers of dirt piled up or as a plunger cleaning the toilet.

koko ここ here

Your ***cocoa*** *is here, said the barista at Starbucks.*

kore これ this (one)

This is the ***core*** *of the matter.*

kotae 答え / こたえ answer

Kotex *is the answer to many a woman's need..*

答 The kanji has the "bamboo" radical ⺮ on top, since early Chinese writing was on bamboo before the invention of paper. Below the bamboo is the kanji 一 for "one" above a mouth (口), under a roof. When a response to a letter is given, figuratively speaking it's a single mouth uttering a message in an indoor space.

kowai 怖い / こわい scary; frightening

When you see a pair of ***cow eyes*** *staring at you up close, it can be very scary. Especially if the cow is a bull!*

怖 The kanji has the "heart" radical 忄 on the left, found in kanji having to do with thought or emotions. The phonetic on the right shows several fingers of the hand clutching a piece of cloth (巾). When something is frightening, we may wipe away our perspiration with a cloth handkerchief!

kuchi 口 / くち mouth

*It's not polite to go up to an adult, tickle them on the chin, and mouth the words "**koochie, koochie, koo**"!*

口 This kanji was originally drawn as a circle, representing the human mouth.

kurai 暗い / くらい dark

*We all sometimes **cry** in the dark.*

暗 The kanji has the "sun" radical 日 on the left, symbolizing light. Darkness is the absence of light. The phonetic on the right shows the sun going down below the horizon at the end of the day. It's actually the kanji 音 for "sound," which is a distortion of the kanji 言, showing sound emanating from the mouth. Sounds in the dark are often scary and might make you cry! The kanji 音 is found in the kanji compound for music, 音楽 (*ongaku*), and thus denotes the onyomi *an* for 暗.

kurasu 暮らす / くらす stay/live somewhere

*When we temporarily have no place to stay, we **crash** at a friend's place.*

暮 This kanji has the "grass/flower" radical 艹 on the top, perhaps referring to the thatched roofs of peasant homes in ancient China. Beneath that is the kanji for sun 日, and the very bottom of the kanji shows the sun rising up. All life depends on the sun, after all.

kuruma 車 / くるま car

***Car room**, and the amount of it, is a priority for large families when buying a car.*

車 The kanji shows a cart or carriage, with the top and bottom horizontal strokes representing the wheels, the long vertical stroke showing the axle, and the middle section portraying the body of the cart, all from a bird's-eye view.

kusuri 薬 / くすり medicine

*You take medicine **'cause you're** sick.*

薬 This kanji has the "grass/flower" radical 艹 on the top, which is the radical for flowers, vegetables, and herbs. Traditional Chinese medicine has been based on herbal remedies for millennia. The phonetic on the bottom is the kanji 楽, which means both "music" and "joy." Music is a wonderful tonic, and when medicine cures you, it is surely a reason for joy. 楽 is a simplification of the traditional kanji for "music" as well as for "joy" (樂), still used in Taiwan and Hong Kong and by Chinese in the West. It shows two bells surrounding a drum on top, placed on a platform made of wood (木), which portrays ancient Chinese music. Music is a great source of enjoyment, said Confucius, and so this kanji also came to mean "enjoyable; pleasurable" when not in combination with other kanji. The simplification in modern Japanese replaces the bells on either side of the drum with what appear to be sound waves emanating from the drum.

kuuki 空気 / くうき air

*Those who sky dive through the air seem to most of us to be **kooky**!*

Literally: "empty air."

空 This kanji, meaning "empty," has the "cave" radical 穴 on top, consisting of a roof with eaves, with the two slanted lines below the roof showing the concavity of the cave. The phonetic is 工, which shows a carpenter's rule for drawing straight lines, with the vertical line in the middle being the handle.

気 This kanji, meaning "air," shows air rising (气) from a certain place (メ).

kyoo 今日 / きょう today

***Oh**, I'm all **keyed** up about **today**!*

Literally: "present day."

今 This kanji means "the present"; "now." The original pictograph was a bell, which was beaten to call the troops to assemble and be all present. It was simplified several thousand years ago and now more resembles a shelter under which is the mallet used to strike the bell.

日 This kanji means "the sun" as well as "day." It was originally a circle with a dot in the middle, indicating the sun, the rising and setting of which divides day from night.

machi 町 / まち town

*In Japan in previous centuries buildings were all made of wood. If someone carelessly threw away a lit **match**, the whole **town** could be burned up.*

町 The kanji has the "field" radical 田 on the left, which shows the square boundaries of the field, with the intersecting lines in the middle depicting the irrigation ditches. The element on the right of 町, namely 丁, shows a "nail" or "tack," with the top horizontal stroke depicting the head of the nail, and the vertical line with the small hook on the end portraying the body of the nail and its sharp point. To remember the kanji 町, think of 丁 as representing the tall buildings in a town, outside of the fields (田).

mae 前 / まえ front

*When I travel I always keep my wallet in **my** front pocket.*

前 The top of the kanji seems to show the two feet of a thief, who creeps into a bank or house at night under the moon (月) while holding a knife, represented by the character on the bottom right. The original pictograph actually showed a boat (舟) in front of the shore. The two strokes to the right of it depict waves, and the two strokes on top of the character show grass growing along the shore.

mame 豆 / まめ beans; peas

*My **Mommy** made me eat my beans and peas when I was young.*

豆 This kanji originally meant a ritual vessel used in ancient China in sacrifices to the spirits of one's ancestors. The top stroke shows the lid of the vessel, with what looks like the "mouth" radical 口 showing the mouth, i.e., opening, of the vessel. The bottom three strokes depict the base of the vessel. This kanji was later borrowed for its sound in Chinese to represent the generic term for "beans" and "peas." It was a clever choice, since the kanji somewhat resembles a bean plant, with the "mouth" depicting the bean pod and the three bottom strokes the vine growing out of the ground.

manabu 学ぶ / まなぶ learn; study

*When you need to learn something difficult, you just have to **man up**!*

学 The kanji is a simplification used in Japan and China after WWII of the original kanji 學 still used in Taiwan and Hong Kong and by Chinese in the West. The original shows two hands on either side of the top part, passing down knowledge (the two Xs) to the student below, who is like a child (子) in his or her ignorance. The roof over the child's head seems to represent the confines of the student's mind. The purpose of study is to remove the roof, i.e., the barrier to learning, and allow true knowledge to enter. The simplified version, also used in mainland China, reduces the entire top half of the character to three simple strokes.

masumasu ますます increasingly

As an object traveling through space accelerates, it increasingly gains ***mass****. Or, as we say in Spanish,* ***más y más*** *(more and more).*

mata また again

The ***mata****dor again killed another bull in the ring.*

mei めい niece

"That's ***me*** *niece," said the man with the Cockney accent.*

mijikai 短い / みじかい short (in length)

A ***midget*** *car is short.*

短 The kanji has the "arrow" radical on the left side, with a kanji showing a ritual vessel, a pot or goblet, on the right. The actual etymology is that these were two relatively short objects in the ancient world.

mimasu 診ます / みます examine a patient

*Grammatically challenged doctors will often say "****me must*** *examine the patient!"*

診 The kanji has the "speech" radical 言 on the left, showing breath coming out of a mouth on the bottom. After examining a patient, a doctor will, of course, pronounce his/her diagnosis. The phonetic on the right of 診 shows shadowing and looks a bit like the lines on an X-ray.

mimi 耳 / みみ ear

*Opera singers warm up by singing arpeggios with the sounds "**mi, mi, mi, mi, mi, mi, mi**." Given the volume of an opera singer's voice, it can be heard by the ear of anyone in the next room.*

耳 The kanji is a depiction of the ear lobe.

mina 皆 / みな all; everyone

*There may be days when it seems everyone we encounter is really **mean**.*

皆 The kanji has two people on top, sitting facing to the right, representing a large number of people. The kanji 白 on the bottom shows a mouth filled with talk (曰), rather than meaning "white" as it normally does. However, as a mnemonic device think about how all brides in the U.S. wear a white wedding dress, at least if it's their first marriage.

minami 南 / みなみ south

Miami *is in the south of the U.S.*

南 The kanji shows plants proliferating in the warm climate of the south, according to the *Shuowen Jiezi*, a 2nd-century Chinese etymological text. However, it looks rather like a cactus under the roof of a greenhouse, which has an antenna on top. A greenhouse, of course, is used in northern latitudes to recreate the warm temperatures of a southern clime.

minikui 醜い / みにくい ugly

In Snow White, *the* ***meanie queen*** *is ugly when she appears in disguise at Snow White's door with the poison apple.*

醜 The kanji has the "devil" radical 鬼 on the right. Originally 鬼 meant "ghost," a meaning it still retains in Chinese, while in both Chinese and Japanese it's also come to mean "demon; devil." And a devil is what this kanji most closely resembles! It has a horn on top of an ugly face with crisscross lines (田), and two legs on the bottom with what appears to be a tail on the bottom right. The 2nd-century Chinese etymological text *Shuowen Jiezi* believed it indicated the whirling motion of a ghost or demon. The phonetic of the kanji 醜 for "ugly" is the kanji 酒 for "alcohol" minus the "water" radical 氵 on the left and shows a bottle with a lid on top. Perhaps this phonetic is appropriate, since many people turn ugly after they've drunk too much alcohol.

miru 見る / みる see

Every day we see ourselves in the ***mirror****.*

The *-masu* form of *miru* is *mimasu.* Think about you really wanting to see something and saying "me must see it!"

見 The kanji shows an eye on two legs.

mise 店 / みせ store

That young ***miss*** *works as a clerk in a store.*

店 This kanji shows the roof and side wall of a store (广). The phonetic under the roof shows the mouth of a fortune teller on the bottom who would read the cracks in a tortoise shell to foretell the future (占). However, 占 looks a bit like a sign pointing to women's blouses or men's slacks in the store.

mitsukeru 見つける / みつける find

*When you want to find something you lost and **care** about, you will do what you can to get your **mitts** on it again.*

見 The kanji shows an eye on two legs. By itself it means "see; meet," but with the addition of つける it means "find." つける means "attach" or "fasten." 見つける therefore implies attaching or fixing your gaze to find something.

mizu 水 / みず water

*If you go too long without drinking water, you'll be pretty **mis**erable!*

水 The kanji was derived from the pictograph for river, 川, which shows water streaming down a riverbed. To create a separate kanji for "water," the ancient Chinese skewed the two outside lines.

mochiron もちろん of course

*When something is delicious, of course we **munch on**.*

monku 文句 / もんく complaint

*If you had to live the spartan life of an ascetic **monk**, you, too, would complain!*

Literally: "sentence-phrase"; this is a transliteration of a Japanese word into kanji, with only tangential relationship to the meaning of the kanji)

文 This kanji originally meant "language." The crossed lines depict written language. It has come to mean "sentence" in modern Japanese as well.

句 This kanji means "phrase," i.e., part of a sentence. What appears to be a hook around a small box is breath emanating from a mouth, which is the essence of speaking.

muzukashii 難しい / むずかしい difficult; hard

Putting on a ***muzzle she*** *finds quite difficult.*

難 The right side of the kanji is the "short-tailed bird" radical. The left side of the kanji is a phonetic. It shows a cow's head on top, a distortion of a rice field (田) below that, with the kanji 大 for "big" on the bottom. The idea is that it is hard for the birds to survive when the fields turn the color of a cow's hide, i.e., brown.

nabe 鍋 / なべ pot

Cooking pots often have ***knobs*** *on the end, to make them easier to grasp.*

鍋 This kanji is used in Chinese for the wok, the main cooking "pot" in preparing Chinese food. In Japanese it refers instead to the Japanese cooking pot, as in the term *nabemono* (鍋物). The kanji 鍋 has the "gold/metal" radical 釒 on the left, used in words for things made out of metal, like the Chinese wok and Japanese cooking pots. The "gold/metal" radical has the "earth" radical on the bottom, with the two short skewed lines on either side of it being nuggets of gold in the earth. The top lines show the gold buried under the ground. The phonetic on the right side of the kanji 鍋 is what appears to be a two-story building but is actually the "bone" radical 骨. Think about bones being cooked along with the meat in the pot.

nado など etc.; and so forth

Rather than giving too many examples of something and have our listeners ***nod off****, we say "etc."*

nagame 眺め / ながめ view

If I get us a hotel room without a view, my wife ***nags at me*** *until I ask for another room.*

眺 The kanji has the "eye" radical 目 on the left. The phonetic on the right seems to indicate looking off in all directions. It actually depicts wooden lots being cast in a Buddhist temple to seek answers to one's prayers. When we go to a beautiful scenic place, we all pray for our hotel room to have a great view, preferably in all directions.

naka 中 / なか inside

I hear something ***knocking*** *about inside the hood of my old car.*

中 The vertical line in this kanji shows an arrow striking right inside the middle of the target.

nakusu なくす lose (something)

Whenever I lose something important, like the car keys or my credit card, I take a lot of ***knocks*** *from my wife!*

nani 何 / なに what?

When Shakespeare's characters sing, "Hey, ***nonny, nonny,****" modern audiences ask, "What?!"*

何 The kanji has the "person" radical 亻 on the left, since it is people who always ask, "What?" Dogs or cats will simply just ignore it, or eat it! The phonetic 可 on the right, meaning "permitted," shows the mouth with breath rising up as someone asks permission for something. It's as if the other person asks, "What?!"

natsu 夏 / なつ summer

Summer is the time to sit in the yard drinking beer and eating ***nuts*** *(ナッツ).*

夏 The kanji shows the head of a farmer on top (頁) and two arms crossed on the bottom. As the 2nd-century Chinese etymological text *Shuowen Jiezi* explains, in summer the farmers are temporarily idle, with their arms hanging by their sides, since the crops they planted in spring are not yet ready to be harvested.

naze なぜ why?

Why does the ***nozzle*** *on so many hoses get so easily plugged up?*

neko 猫 / ねこ cat

Cats with their furry coats don't wear clothes, but go around ***naked****.*

猫 The kanji has the "animal" radical 犭 on the left, which is found as the radical in the vast majority of kanji for various mammals, including cats. The phonetic 苗 on the right side, meaning "sprouts," has the "grass/flower" radical 艹 on top and the "field" radical 田 on the bottom. Cats love to cleanse their stomachs by going out into the fields and eating grass, after all.

nemasu 寝ます / ねます sleep

Nay, mus*t sleep, says the tired person asked to do something.*

寝 The kanji has the "roof" radical 宀 on top, seeming to show under the roof a person on the left using his or her hands on the right to lay a child on the bed to sleep at night.

nigeru 逃げる / にげる escape

Negro *slaves in the old South would try to escape whenever they could.*

逃 The kanji has the "walk" radical 辶 on the left, since in ancient times the principal way to escape from capture was on foot. The phonetic on the right seems to show prisoners or slaves escaping in all directions. It actually depicts wooden lots being cast in a Buddhist temple to seek an answer to one's prayers. Anyone wishing to escape would, of course, pray for freedom.

niku 肉 / にく meat

When you order meat at the deli, the butcher takes ***nicks*** *out of the meat as he slices it.*

肉 The kanji shows a piece of meat, with the two 人 showing the marbling of the fat in the meat.

nishi 西 / にし west

Nietzsche *was a Western philosopher.*

西 This kanji actually shows the belly and long legs of a sea bird inside its nest. When the sun sets in the west, the birds go to their nests to rest, explains the 2nd-century Chinese etymological text *Shuowen Jiezi*.

nodo のど throat

If a singer uses the throat too much in singing, he or she may develop vocal ***nodes.***

nomimasu 飲みます / のみます drink

*If you do not drink alcohol and your Japanese host offers you beer or sake, you might say "**no, me must** not drink alcohol."*

飲 The kanji has the "food" radical 食 on the left, which shows a hand on top reaching into a rice bowl in the middle and scooping up the rice with a spoon, pictured on the bottom. The right side shows a person on the bottom, with breath rising up, and means "to inhale." When we drink, it is often with food, and we figuratively inhale the beverage.

obaasan おばあさん grandmother [honorific]; grandma

*My **obaasan** makes me wear an **obaakooto** (overcoat) when it's cold outside.*

oboeru 覚える / おぼえる learn; remember; memorize

*I can never learn to play the **oboe**, but I remember it represents the duck in "Peter and the Wolf."*

覚 The kanji is a simplification after WWII of the traditional kanji, 覺. The traditional form, still used in Taiwan and Hong Kong and by Chinese in the West, has the kanji 見, "to see," on the bottom, showing an eye (目) on two legs (儿). We usually need to see something to learn it and remember it. The top part of the traditional kanji shows two hands on either side, passing down knowledge (the 2 Xs) to students, whose minds are restricted in their ignorance as if there were a roof over their minds. Learning removes the roof from the mind of the student and lets in knowledge. The simplified version of the kanji now used in Japan and mainland China only puts three little lines in place of the meaningful top half of the original. Think of those three little lines as the knowledge penetrating the mind of the learner.

ocha お茶 / おちゃ tea

*The caffeine in tea makes you **cha-cha**!*

茶 The kanji for tea has the "grass/flower" radical 艹 found at the top of characters for flowers, vegetables, and herbs. Below the "grass/flower" radical is a shelter under which a large tea plant, represented by the "tree" radical 木, is being dried, before the leaves are plucked off to make tea. The initial お is an honorific put in front of some of the most important items in Japanese daily life, including money (おかね).

odoroku 驚く / おどろく be surprised

*In Japan you will be surprised by many unfamiliar **odors** that **occur**.*

驚 The kanji has the "horse" radical 馬 on the bottom, which shows the mane, body, and four legs of a horse. Horses are easily startled by the slightest noise. The phonetic 敬 on top of the kanji 驚 means "respect." It shows two hands on the right as the radical. Asians will always give and receive everything with two hands, to show respect for the other person. The phonetic on the left of 敬 has the "grass/flower" radical 艹 on top, with the kanji for "phrase" 句 below it, showing breath rising from a mouth. We Americans are often surprised by the high level of respect the Japanese accord other people, as they offer us so many things with both hands, while speaking flowery words that seem very sincere. The Japanese are arguably the world's most polite and gracious people.

odoru 踊る / おどる dance

*Those of us who **adore** dancing must admit that when we dance we do perspire and exude a certain **odor**.*

踊 The kanji has one of the "foot radicals" on the left, since it is with the foot that we dance. This radical is a variation of the kanji 足 (*ashi*) for "foot." In this variation the sole and heel of the foot are raised off the ground, with the vertical stroke representing the leg. The little box on top portrays the contour of the leg, although it looks like the kneecap. Imagine the phonetic 甬 on the right to be a 19th-century Southern belle like Scarlett O'Hara, dancing in a big hoop skirt, with the top two strokes depicting her head.

ogoru おごる treat to food or drink

***Ogres** rarely treat anyone to food or drink, including nice **ogres** like Shrek.*

ohashi お箸 / おはし chopsticks

*Chopsticks are useful in eating many things, including **hash**.*

箸 The kanji has the "bamboo" radical ⺮ on top, since chopsticks were traditionally made of bamboo. The phonetic seems to show the sun on the bottom (日) rising above the earth (土) at the break of day. The Japanese, as well as the Chinese, use chopsticks to eat from the first thing in the morning until late at night.

oi おい nephew

*When you have a young, rambunctious nephew, a Jewish person may utter "**Oy** veh!"*

ojiisan おじいさん grandfather [honorific]; grandpa

***Oh, gee**, grandpa. Thanks so much for the gift!*

okaasan お母さん / おかあさん mother [honorific]

*A mother **cares** about her **son**.*

母 The kanji shows a mother's two breasts, turned 90 degrees to make it easier to write. The breasts refer to the mother nursing an infant.

okane お金 / おかね money

Oh, can I *do a lot of things if only I had the money!*

金 This kanji has the "earth" radical 土 on the bottom, with the two short skewed lines on either side of it being nuggets of gold in the earth. The top lines show the gold buried under the ground.

okiru 起きる / おきる get up

As we get up in the morning, we might notice the ***oak*** *outside our window, which can get up to a great height.*

起 The kanji has the character 走, meaning "to run," on the left, as the radical, which shows a foot on the bottom (止), with the heel and sole of the foot raised, running along the ground (土). The phonetic 己 on the right, depicts a silkworm crawling upward.

okoru 怒る / おこる get angry

Many things ***occur*** *that make us angry.*

怒 The kanji has the "heart" radical 心 on the bottom, found in most characters related to emotions. The phonetic 奴 on top shows a woman on the left being controlled by a hand on the right, and means "slave." The idea of slavery should make us all angry!

oneesan お姉さん / おねえさん older sister [honorific]

*My older sister is always saying to her boyfriend, "****Oh, nay!****"*

姉　The kanji has the "woman" radical 女 on the left. The right side seems to show older sister with her arms held down at her side.

oniisan　お兄さん / おにいさん　older brother [honorific]

*My older brother is much taller than me. I only come up to his **knee**.*

兄　The kanji shows a mouth on two legs. The true etymology of this kanji is that older brother in ancient China was the authority in his generation, and when he spoke, the younger siblings had to listen and obey.

osoi　遅い / おそい　slow; late

*If you're going so slowly, we're going to be **oh so** late!*

遅　The kanji has the "walk" radical 辶 on the left, apropos of walking slowly, with the result that you'll be late. The right side shows a sheep (羊), with its horns on top of the skeins of wool on its body, coming into a shelter, represented by a doorway. Sheep are slow in coming back into their pen after grazing out in the meadow.

otoosan　お父さん / おとうさん　father [honorific]

*My father always says to me, "I **told** you, **son**!"*

父　The kanji, which by itself means "father," shows the father's two hands raised above his head in a gesture of authority.

otooto　弟 / おとうと　younger brother [humble]

*The little train my younger brother plays with goes "**toot**, toot."*

弟　The horns on top of the kanji symbolize power or authority. In traditional Chinese culture the younger brother, being a male, has some authority in the family. The rest of the kanji shows a thread, looking like the "bow" radical 弓, being wound around a bobbin in a loom, represented by the vertical line. The metaphor here is that younger brothers follow the birth of their older brother one after another, just as threads follow one after another as the loom weaves.

otto　夫 / おっと　my husband [humble]

*My husband's name is **Otto**, and he loves his **auto**.*

夫　This kanji shows a powerful person with what appears to be two sets of arms, the better to protect his wife.

oya　親 / おや　my parents [humble]

*Ungrateful children, when it gets to be Mother's Day or Father's Day, will finally say to themselves "**Oh, yeah**, I should do something for my parents."*

親　The kanji actually means "relatives." On the right side it has 見, "to meet" or "to see," as the radical, since relatives are people we see regularly in our lives. The phonetic on the left has the character 立, meaning "to stand," on the top, with the kanji 木 for "tree" on the bottom. Relatives, especially our parents, are people who "stand" in our family tree and whom we see regularly.

oyogimasu　泳ぎます / およぎます　swim

*Should Yogi Bear's companion in the cartoon series, Boo-Boo, see Yogi trapped by the Ranger on the side of a lake, Boo-Boo would probably think to himself, "**Oh, Yogi must** swim!"*

泳　The kanji has the "water" radical 氵 on the left. The phonetic on the right, which means "eternal," has the kanji 水 for "water" on the bottom, with two extra strokes on the top to make it look different The idea here is that water in rivers is perpetually (eternally) flowing.

rei 例 / れい example

Ray *Charles, the famous singer/songwriter is a great example of what a blind person can accomplish with enough talent and hard work.*

例 The kanji has the "person" radical 亻 on the left, since we humans look to great people as examples to follow. The phonetic on the right has the "death" radical 歹 on the left, which depicts a skull, and the "sword" radical 刂 on the right. There are certainly many examples in Shakespeare's plays of characters dying at the hands of a knife or sword.

renshuu 練習 / れんしゅう practice

When a runner practices, he/she must wear ***running shoes.***

Literally: "refine-learn." Often used with *suru.*

練 This kanji means "to refine." It has the "thread" radical 糸 on the left, referring to the refining process required in turning threads from the silkworm cocoons into silk. The original phonetic on the right has been replaced in recent decades with the kanji 東 for "east," which shows the sun (日) coming up over the trees (木) in the east as dawn breaks. Appropriate enough, perhaps, to have the kanji for "east" together with the "thread" radical representing silk since it was in the East that silk was first produced. You refine your knowledge of a subject through practice.

習 This kanji means "to learn." It has two wings (羽) of a bird on top of the kanji 白 for "white." When you are beginning to learn something, you are a "white belt" novice, who is like a fledging bird just learning to fly.

ringo りんご apple

*Fried apple **rings** are delicious! And **Ringo** Starr of the Beatles was rumored to love apples.*

sabishii 寂しい / さびしい sad; lonely

***Sob she** does when she sees a sad movie.*

寂 The kanji has the "roof" radical on top, for it is when we are at home alone that we most often feel lonely and sad. There is a hand (又) on the lower right of the kanji picking beans from the bean stalk on the lower left. Harvesting beans is lonely work, after all. A useful mnemonic device might be to see the bean stalk as a person facing a little table on the right, eating a lonely meal by him- or herself.

sai 歳 / さい years of age

*As our years of age pile up, we may very well **sigh**!*

歳 The kanji has a foot (止) on top and a roof with a side wall (厂) below, under which there is a distortion of the "foot" radical 足 and a halberd (戈). Chinese books on etymology claim that this character originally showed the planet Jupiter, which the Chinese associated with war, much as the Romans did with the planet Mars. Since Jupiter's revolutions around the sun were calculated in years, the character came to mean "years," and, by extension, "years of age." Remember the kanji by thinking that as we get older, time marches on, represented by the feet in the kanji. Figuratively speaking, we may begin to feel more and more wounded in body (the halberd), but hopefully not in spirit.

sakana 魚 / さかな fish

***Sockeye** salmon is one type of fish.*

魚 The ancient version of this kanji showed a fish hanging on a hook. The top few strokes are the head, and the middle part (田) shows the scaly body of the fish rather than a field, with the four strokes on the bottom representing the tail of the fish and not fire. When the ancient Chinese scribes codified the language several thousand years ago, they simplified many pictographs and in so doing made some parts of kanji the same for a number of pictographs that originally had been quite different.

samui 寒い / さむい cold (air temperature)

*Yosemite **Sam** in the Warner Brothers cartoons must be feeling cold, to always be wearing a huge sombrero and keeping his mustache so big and bushy!*

寒 According to the 2nd-century etymological text *Shuowen Jiezi*, this kanji shows a person taking shelter from the cold in a bed of straw under a roof. The "ice" radical 冫 is on the very bottom of the character, with the crossed lines above depicting the straw and with the "roof" radical 宀 on the very top.

sanpo 散歩 / さんぽ walk

*When Brazilians take a walk, they might **samba** a little.*

Literally: "scatter-steps." Often used with *suru*.

散 This kanji means "to scatter." It shows two hands on the right as the radical. The phonetic on the left seems to show little bits of grass on the top with the moon on the bottom. At night little creatures like rabbits scatter about to eat whatever grass they might find.

歩 This kanji means "steps." It shows the foot at rest on the top (止), with the sole and heel of the foot flat. On the bottom the foot is depicted in motion, with the sole and heel of the foot raised as if in mid-step.

sara 皿 / さら plate; dish

*After enjoying a **Sara** Lee cake, you have to wash the plate.*

皿 This kanji is the "dish" radical. To modern eyes it looks a bit like a butter dish, but it was originally written as a circle and was meant to show the inside of a plate.

seifu 政府 / せいふ government

*We expect our government to keep us **safe**.*

Literally: "political/administrative-residence."

政 This kanji means "political; govern." It has the "double hands" radical 攵 on the right side, as a metaphor for the government managing administrative affairs. The phonetic on the left side is the kanji 正, which means "straight; upright; just; correct." 正 shows the foot at rest (止), with the sole of the foot flat on the ground at the bottom, stopping just at a certain spot, represented by the top horizontal line (一). This phonetic was perhaps chosen in the hope that government would be upright and just.

府 This kanji means "official residence" or "mansion." It is written with the radical 广, which shows a roof with a single roof tile and a side wall. The phonetic inside, 付, means "to pay." It shows a person on the left paying money with the hand pictured on the right (寸). Since citizens all have to pay taxes to their government, the choice of phonetic seems significant. And because those who are in power in any government live in a special official residence, the compound word for "government" in Chinese literally means "political mansion" or "official residence of those who govern."

seiji 政治 / せいじ politics

*There are all too few **sages** in politics!*

Literally: "political-rule."

政　This kanji means "political; govern." It has the "double hands" radical 攵 on the right side, as a metaphor for the government managing administrative affairs. The phonetic on the left side is the kanji 正, which means "straight; upright; just; correct." 正 shows the foot at rest (止), with the sole of the foot flat on the ground at the bottom, stopping just at a certain spot, represented by the top horizontal line (一). This phonetic was perhaps chosen in the hope that government would be upright and just.

治　This kanji means "to rule," as well as "cure; heal." It has the "water" radical 氵 on the left side, perhaps chosen because all ancient civilizations, including China, developed centralized governments through the need to organize large irrigation projects for agricultural production. On the right side of the kanji is the nose and mouth of a governing official. Since the kanji 治 also means "cure; heal," a useful mnemonic is to think of it as showing the fluids (water) in the nose and mouth that we experience when we suffer the common cold and are in need of a cure.

sekai　世界 / せかい　world

Christians believe that Jesus died for the ***sake*** *of the* *world.*

Literally: "generation-boundary."

世　This kanji is a shorthand version of 三十, meaning "thirty," and by itself means "a generation," since a new generation is born every thirty years or so. Although there are a lot more than thirty countries in the world today, think of this kanji as representing the great multitude of nations in the world.

界　This kanji has the "field" radical 田 on top. From an agricultural perspective, the world is just one big field for raising crops. The phonetic 介 on the bottom means "to introduce." It shows two people meeting under a roof. If we could introduce everyone in the world to one another, perhaps then we'd have a chance for world peace!

seki 席 / せき seat

*Trains and buses provide seats for the **sake** of their passengers.*

席 The kanji has the "roof with wall" radical 广, since most seats are indoors. Under the roof there appears to be a person sitting on a stool.

sekken せっけん soap

*For the **sake** of others, always use soap when you shower!*

semai 狭い / せまい narrow

***Say, my**, that passage is narrow!*

狭 The kanji has the "animal" radical 犭 on the left, since dogs can creep into places too narrow for humans. The phonetic on the right contributes to this meaning by showing a person holding two small objects by pressing his arms down close to his body.

senmon 専門 / せんもん specialty

*When you major in a subject in college you generally take more than one **seminar** in your speciality.*

Literally: "special-door."

専 This kanji means "special; exclusive." According to the Chinese etymological text of 1,800 years ago, the *Shuowen Jiezi,* it represents the yoke put around the head of an ox, which was the special/exclusive way to get the ox to pull a cart. A more helpful mnemonic, perhaps, is to see this kanji as a distortion of the kanji 車 for "cart/car," with the bottom wheel missing. Therefore it will exclusively/only go if pushed by hand (寸).

門 This kanji means "door; gate." It shows the traditional Chinese/Japanese door or gate, which was made of two large pieces of wood that were pushed open and closed. This kanji is used metaphorically in some kanji compounds, a reference to the door of learning through which a student must pass.

sensei 先生 / せんせい teacher

*Hopefully your Japanese teacher is **sensa**tional.*

Literally: "first-born."

先 This kanji means "first." It shows a person walking along, with the line on the top left indicating that he/she is in the lead, even if it does look a bit like a baton twirler going first in front of a marching band. Be aware that when the pictograph 土 appears at the top of a kanji, it depicts the head of a person, and not "earth" or "dirt."

生 This kanji means "to give birth to." It represents a plant coming out of the ground, bearing (giving birth to) a blossom, which is shown by the slanted stroke on the top left.

sensoo 戦争 / せんそう war

*The people of a country become in**censed**, **so** they go to war.*

Literally: "war-struggle" or "war-dispute."

戦 This kanji means "war." It has the "halberd" radical 戈 on the right, a common weapon in ancient China. The phonetic 単 on the left was slightly simplified after WWII from its original form, 單, which shows two mouths on top and a pitchfork on the bottom. By itself it has come to mean "single" and is derived from the idea of assailing an enemy in single-hand combat with loud cries and a pitchfork. This is another case where the phonetic also contributes to the meaning.

争 This kanji means "to struggle; to dispute." The top two strokes depict the hand of a person reaching for a dagger, represented by the single vertical line, while another person reaches for it with his hand, depicted by the three horizontal strokes (ヨ).

sentaku 洗濯 / せんたく laundry

When I was richer, I always ***sent out*** *my* *laundry* *to be washed.*

Literally: "wash-clean," i.e., a redundant compound.

洗 This kanji means "to wash." It has the "water" radical 氵 on the left, logically enough. The phonetic on the right side, pronounced *sen* in *sentaku* (洗濯 "laundry"), is also the *sen* in *sensei* (先生 "teacher"). 先 looks a bit like a person carrying a bath towel into the bathroom to wash up.

濯 This kanji is mostly used as the suffix in the compound 洗濯. Like 洗, it has the "water" radical 氵 on the left. On the bottom right is the "short-tailed bird" radical 隹, with its two wings pictured on top. Birds need to clean their feathers regularly, which is why many of us put bird baths out for them.

setsumei 説明 / せつめい explanation

In giving an explanation, I always declare "so ***says me****."*

Literally: "speak-clearly."

説 This kanji means "speak; say" but in Japanese has come to mean "explain" or "preach." It has the "speech" radical 言 on the left, appropriately enough. On the right side is the classical Chinese word for "older brother," 兄, with what resembles horns on top symbolizing authority. When older brother speaks, his younger siblings have to listen.

明 This kanji originally meant "bright" but has come to mean "clear; obvious" in Japanese. It has the "sun" on the left and the "moon" on the right. Both of these heavenly bodies appear as bright, clear lights in the sky.

shaberu しゃべる chat; talk

*When we chat with our colleagues, we often talk **shop**.*

A bit less formal than *hanasu*, just as in English "chat" or "talk" is a bit less formal than "converse" or "speak."

shakai 社会 / しゃかい society

*Some of the things we notice about Japanese society, as well as our own society, may be **shocking**.*

Literally: "society-assembly."

社 This kanji means "society." It has the "god" radical ネ on the left, with the kanji for "earth" on the right. The true etymology is that it represents the emperor praying to God every year for a good harvest on behalf of the entire society.

会 This kanji means "meeting; gathering." Under a roof is the character for "two" above the outline of a nose. It seems to be showing two noses, representing two people, meeting under a roof. After all, two nose (knows) better than one! The truth is that this kanji is a simplification used in both China and Japan after WWII of the kanji 會, still used in Taiwan and Hong Kong and by Chinese in the West, which shows two people talking in a doorway under a roof. The 日 on the bottom represents a mouth filled with talk, rather than the sun.

shashin 写真 / しゃしん photograph

*Printed photos are glossy and **so shiny**!*

Literally: "copy-reality."

写 This kanji means "to write" in Chinese. However, in Japanese it has come to mean "to copy something," either by writing, drawing, or by using some kind of equipment such as a camera. It is the simplified version used in Japan and mainland China since the 1950s of the original kanji 寫, which shows a magpie under a roof. The original concept of this word was that the magpie is a bird that makes its nest in a very orderly, neat fashion. Likewise, those who write should carefully order their thoughts before putting them down on paper. The kanji looks a bit like a student writing a term paper on a computer under a roof, with the head directly below the roof and the fingers on the keyboard at the very bottom of the character. The simplified version used now is a bare-bones outline and removes the roof tile on top of the original kanji.

真 This kanji means "real; true." It has the kanji for "ten" 十 above the kanji for "eye" 目, on top of a simple diagram of a stand or table. The actual metaphor was that if something is indeed true, then you could put it up high for ten eyes, i.e., a large number of people, to be able to see that it is true.

shi 詩 / し poem

*Emily Dickinson, **she** wrote many beautiful **poems.***

The kanji has the "speech" radical 言 on the left, showing breath rising up from a mouth (口). Poems are meant to be read aloud. The phonetic for 詩 is the kanji 寺 for "Buddhist temple." It has the "earth" radical 土 on the top, which shows something sitting on the ground, with the kanji for "inch" 寸 on the bottom, which shows a hand with thumb and forefinger extended. The emperor bestowed (寸) land (土) to the Buddhist temples. Although the phonetic was not necessarily intended to contribute to the meaning, it is true that in both China and Japan there were some Buddhist monks who wrote some notable poetry.

shiai 試合 / しあい game; match

***She and I** watch a lot of soccer **games** together.*

Literally: "test–join together."

試 This kanji means "to try; to try out (something); to test." It has the "speech" radical 訁 on the left, since often tests are given orally. The phonetic on the right shows a carpenter's rule on the bottom left (工) with a dart or small arrow (弋) on the right. The character 式 means "style," with the idea being that weapons are made in a certain style or form according to certain measurements, using a carpenter's rule. Every test is given in a certain style or manner, and the mettle of any team is tested in a game according to certain rules.

合 This kanji has the "mouth" radical 口 on the bottom, with the triangle at the top representing a joining together. The actual etymology is the coming together of many people to discuss something and reach an accord. A game is a contest in which opponents join together to decide which side is the winner.

shigoto 仕事 / しごと job; work

*The job of shepherds is to care for **she-goats** and male goats.*

Literally: "serving-affairs."

仕 This kanji means "to serve (someone)." It has the "person" radical 亻 on the left, with the kanji for "scholar" 士 on the right as a meaningful phonetic. The scholar is shown standing with arms stretched out in a gesture of authority. Scholars in ancient China served as government officials.

事 This kanji means "occurrence" or "affair" and shows a hand, represented by the horizontal lines, grasping a brush and writing things down.

shiken 試験 / しけん test

***She can** pass the test, but I can't.*

Literally: "try-examine."

試 This kanji means "to try" or "to try out (something)." Tests try out or test your ability at a subject. The kanji has the "speech" radical 言 on the left, since tests are often given orally. The phonetic on the right shows a carpenter's rule on the bottom left (工) with a dart or small arrow (弋) on the right. The kanji 式 means "style," with the idea being that weapons are made in a certain style or form according to certain measurements, using the carpenter's rule. Every test is given in a certain style or manner, after all.

験 This kanji means "examine." It has the "horse" radical 馬 on the left. Before buying a horse, the buyer will carefully examine the horse to determine the age and condition of the animal. The phonetic on the right, which was simplified in the 20th century, seems to show a person in a hat striding toward the horse to examine it.

shima 島 / しま island

The islands of the Caribbean ***shimmer*** *in the sun.*

島 The kanji shows a bird (鳥) perched on a spit of land that sticks out from the sea like a mountain (山).

shimasu します do

She must *do it!*

shinbun 新聞 / しんぶん newspaper

The newspaper boy got bitten on the ***shinbone*** *by the resident dog.*

Literally: "newly-heard."

新 This kanji has the "axe" radical on the right, showing the handle on the bottom right and the blade of the axe on the top and left side. The actual idea was that in order to make a new home for yourself, you have to hew wooden beams with an axe. The phonetic 亲 on the left meaning "relative" seems to contribute to the meaning. It's written with the kanji 立 meaning "to stand" on the top, and the kanji 木 for "tree" on the bottom. When you use an axe to make a new home for yourself, you must first cut down the trees standing there to clear a space.

聞　This kanji meaning "to hear" shows an ear (耳) in a doorway (門).

shinpu　新婦 / しんぷ　bride

Being a bride is not that ***simple****, given all there is to plan for a wedding.*

Literally: "new-wife."

新　This kanji has the "axe" radical on the right, showing the handle on the bottom right and the blade of the axe on the top and left side. The actual idea was that in order to make a new home for yourself, you have to hew wooden beams with an axe. The phonetic 亲 on the left meaning "relative" seems to contribute to the meaning. It's written with the kanji 立 meaning "to stand" on the top, and the kanji 木 for "tree" on the bottom. When you use an axe to make a new home for yourself, you must first cut down the trees standing there to clear a space.

婦　This kanji for "wife" has the "woman" radical 女 on the left. The right side shows a hand on top holding a cloth duster (巾) under the roof of the home. Remember that Chinese men made up these kanji two to three millennia ago.

shinpu　神父 / しんぷ　Catholic priest

Catholic priests devote themselves to God and a ***simple*** *life, especially those who are monks.*

Literally: "God-father," i.e., "Holy-Father."

神 The kanji has the "god" radical ネ on the left. When this radical appears on the left of a kanji, it looks a bit like a man in a necktie, turning to the right and heading to church. In reality it's a deliberate distortion of an altar (示) on which something (一) is placed on top as an offering to God. The phonetic on the right side of 神 has a vertical line extending out from a farmer's field (田) and means "to extend." God extends his bounty to us, including the bounty of the fields.

父 This kanji, which by itself means "father," shows the father's two hands raised above his head in a gesture of authority.

shinseki 親戚 / しんせき relatives

*Since we often brush **shins** with our relatives at Thanksgiving and Christmas, for the **sake** of peace in the family we should always be kind to them.*

Literally: "relative-relation," i.e., a redundant compound.

親 This kanji means "relative." On the right side it has the radical 見, "to meet" or "to see," since relatives are people we see regularly in our lives. The phonetic on the left has the character 立 meaning "to stand" on the top, with the kanji 木 for "tree" on the bottom. Relatives are people who "stand" in our family tree and whom we see regularly.

戚 This kanji also means "relative" or "relations" It seems to show our desire to protect our relatives, who are part of our family tree or plant (朩), by sheltering them under our roof (厂) and defending them with weapons (戈) if necessary.

shinshitsu 寝室 / しんしつ bedroom

*The bedroom is where we rest our **shins** on the **sheets** of our bed, along with the rest of us.*

Literally: "sleeping-room."

寝　This kanji has the "roof" radical 宀 on top, and below it seems to be a person on the left using his or her hands on the right to lay a child on the bed to sleep at night.

室　This kanji also has the "roof" radical 宀 on top. The phonetic below the roof shows a bird nosediving down to a place on the ground (土).

shiroi　白い / しろい　white

*Those sheets are **sheer** white.*

白　The kanji shows the sun (日) at dawn, with the slanted stroke at the top showing the rising of the sun. Hence the whiteness of dawn.

shita　下 / した　under; below

*When something drops under the table, some of us may be heard to utter "oh, **shit**a!"*

下　The vertical and slanted lines of this kanji point downward from the horizontal stroke on top, which represents the ground.

shitsumon　質問 / しつもん　question

*I don't understand! Oh, **shitsu**! **Mon** dieu! I have a question!*

Literally: "quality-ask," i.e., ask the quality of something.

質　This kanji has two axes (斤) on top, used for their sound to represent the Chinese measurement fairly equivalent to the English "pound." The bottom of the kanji has the "shell/money" radical 貝. The price a buyer pays for something is based on the quality or nature of the item.

問　The kanji has the "mouth" radical 口 in the middle of the "door" radical 門 in this kanji that combines two radicals and has no phonetic. When someone knocks on our door, we ask "Who's there?"

shitsurei 失礼 / しつれい rudeness

Saying ***"shit" sure*** *is rude!*

Literally: "lose-etiquette)

失 This kanji means "to lose." It shows a person with arms outstretched (夫) having something drop from his hand, hence the meaning of "to lose."

礼 This kanji means "ritual; etiquette." It has the "god" radical ネ on the left, which looks like a man in a necktie headed to church but is really a distortion of an altar on which to lay sacrifices to the spirits (示). The right side is a hook, since God "hooks" us, i.e., draws us to Himself, through ritual. The truth is that this kanji is a simplification of the original kanji, 禮; on the right the two hands on top laying a ritual vessel on the altar are a phonetic that contributes to the meaning. This original kanji is still used in Taiwan and Hong Kong and by Chinese in the West.

shokuyoku 食欲 / しょくよく appetite

The huge appetite of some people will ***shock you.***

Literally: "eating-desire."

食 This kanji means "eat." It shows a hand on top reaching in to a rice bowl in the middle and scooping up the rice with a spoon, pictured on the bottom.

欲 This kanji means "desire." The radical on the right side shows a person on the bottom, with breath rising up. When we really desire something, we tend to breathe heavily.
The phonetic in this kanji is on the left side. The two sets of slanted lines at the top indicate the folds of a mountain valley, with the small box on the bottom not a mouth but rather the

valley itself. However, it looks to me like a gentleman with slanted eyes and a mustache, with his mouth open in desire.

shoobai 商売 / しょうばい business

*Business is all about **showing** the customer something, hoping he or she will **buy** it.*

Literally: "commercial-selling."

商 This kanji means "commerce." It shows a merchant, with the top two strokes depicting his head; below this his two legs appear to be inside his store or place of business. The small mouth on the bottom (口) represents his calling out to passersby to attract their attention and get their business.

売 This kanji means "to sell." It is a simplification used after WWII for the traditional kanji 賣 still used in Taiwan and Hong Kong and by the Chinese in the West. The original kanji uses the kanji 買 meaning "to buy" on the bottom, since someone buying his product is the result the seller is seeking. The kanji 買 shows a net on the top, with the "shell" radical symbolizing money on the bottom. In ancient China, cowry shells were used as currency, so you would have to scoop up a bunch of them to go make a purchase. The top part of the traditional kanji 賣 shows the outstretched arms of the seller, changing the kanji "to buy" to the kanji "to sell." In the simplified version of the kanji now used in Japan, 売, the seller with outstretched arms remains, but on the bottom his two legs are depicted below the roof of his store.

shookai 紹介 / しょうかい introduction

*When introduced to a Japanese person, you ask yourself, "**Should I** bow or **shake** hands?"*

Literally: "introduce-introduce." Often used with *suru*.

紹 This kanji has the "thread" radical 糸 on the left. The phonetic on the right shows a knife (刀) above a mouth (口). When a new official was presented to the emperor, he was given bolts of silk, a sword, and congratulatory words.

介 This kanji shows two people being introduced to one another under a slanted roof.

shoorai 将来 / しょうらい the future

*"**Show I** the future," says the grammatically challenged person to a fortune teller.*

Literally: "take [what's] coming."

将 This kanji was the classical word meaning "to take." The traditional version of the kanji is 將. It has the "left side" radical on the left, looking like a table or altar, but which actually shows the left half of a split log from which altars might be made. The right side shows a piece of meat (a deliberate distortion of the "meat" radical 月, which itself is a simplification of the kanji 肉 for "meat") being placed on an altar by a hand (寸) as an offering to the spirits of the ancestors. In its simplified version 将, used since the 1950s in both Japan and mainland China, the altar on the left is rendered in a more skeletal outline and the piece of meat on the top right is replaced by a hand reaching in and supporting the hand on the bottom right.

来 This kanji means "to come." It's the simplified form of the kanji 來, in which the "tree" radical 木 represents a large grain plant that has borne several ears of wheat or millet, represented by the two small 人. To the ancient Chinese who lived in a largely agricultural society, they thought of the idea of "coming" in terms of the coming of the harvest. The current form of the kanji, 来, used since the 1950s in both Japan and mainland China, replaces the two small "people radicals" with what appear to be two grains of wheat or millet.

shoosetsu 小説 / しょうせつ novel

*A novel **shows sets** of characters to the reader.*

Literally: "small-talk," showing the traditional contempt by Chinese scholars for fiction as opposed to philosophy, which they perceived to be much more profound.)

小 This kanji means "small." It shows a person with arms down by his or her side, looking small.

説 This kanji means "speak." It has the "speech" radical on the left, appropriately enough. On the right side is the classical Chinese word for "older brother," 兄, with what resembles horns on top and represents authority. When older brother speaks, his younger siblings have to listen.

shooten 商店 / しょうてん store

*Stores **show ten**, if not hundreds, of items for sale.*

Literally "commercial-store." More common in writing, while *mise* is the more common spoken word.

商 This kanji means "commerce." It shows a merchant, with the top two strokes depicting his head, below which his two legs appear to be inside his store or place of business. The small mouth on the bottom (口) represents his calling out to passersby to attract their attention and get their business.

店 This kanji shows the roof and side wall of a store (广). The phonetic under the roof shows at the bottom the mouth of a fortune teller, who reads the cracks in a tortoise shell to foretell the future (占). However, 占 looks a bit like a sign pointing to women's blouses or men's slacks in the store.

shukudai 宿題 / しゅくだい homework

*When I tell my students that doing a lot of homework won't kill them, they reply, "**Sure you could die**!"*

Literally: "home-questions."

宿 This character means "to stay overnight; dwelling." It has the "person" radical 亻 and the character 百 for "one hundred" under a roof. The original idea was an inn or similar lodging where a large number of people can spend the night. Think of the person on the bottom left of the kanji as being a student who has been assigned one hundred problems as homework.

題 This kanji means "questions; problems." It has the "head" radical 頁 on the right, which is the part of the body we use to figure out problems, after all. The phonetic 是 on the left side originally meant "correct" but is now used in modern Chinese as the verb "to be." The kanji shows a person (人) under (下) the sun (日). When you're a human being existing under the sun, you've inevitably got a lot of questions and problems, even if they're not all in the form of homework!

shumi 趣味 / しゅみ hobby

*So **sue me**, but I want to spend time on my hobby.*

Literally: "interest-flavor."

趣 This kanji means "interest" in something. It has the radical 走 on the left, whose original meaning was "to go." 走 shows the foot in motion on the bottom, with the sole and heel of the foot raised in walking on the ground, pictured on top (土). On the right side of 趣 is the element 取, which depicts a hand on the right (又) seizing an ear of someone (耳) and means "to take; seize." When our interest in something is aroused, it is as if we are seized by it, and our activities then go in that direction as we pursue it as a hobby.

味 This kanji means "flavor; taste." It has the "mouth" radical 口 on the left. The phonetic 未 on the right means "not yet" and shows a tree (木) whose top branch, represented by the top horizontal line, is not yet fully grown out. Every hobby has its own "flavor" that attracted us to it, even if our expertise in it has not yet grown to the level of an expert.

shutchoo 出張 / しゅっちょう business trip

Business people go on business trips to ***search out*** *new clients.*

Literally: "go out-expand."

出 This kanji means "to go out." It shows a plant coming out of the ground.

張 This kanji means "to stretch; expand." It has the "bow" radical 弓 on the left. The phonetic 長 on the right is the kanji for "long." The top of this kanji depicts long flowing hair, tied by a hair ornament that is displayed on the bottom. The idea behind the kanji 張, therefore, is to expand or extend something, just as the archer stretches out his bowstring and makes it longer.

shuukan 習慣 / しゅうかん custom; habit

Sure you can *do it, if it's the custom.*

Literally: "learned-habit."

習 This kanji means "to learn." On top it shows the two wings of a fledging bird (羽) just learning to fly. The bottom of the kanji looks like the pictograph 白 for "white" but originally showed the body of the little bird. A helpful mnemonic might be to think of the little bird learning to fly as a "white belt," i.e., novice, at flying.

慣 This kanji means "habit/accustomed to." It has the "heart" radical 忄 on the left, which also represents "the mind" in so many kanji. Our habits are formed mentally, after all. The phonetic on the right shows a string of cowry shells (貝), which the ancient Chinese were accustomed to using as currency before the invention of copper coins and paper money.

shuumatsu 週末 / しゅうまつ weekend

*We particularly need **shoe mats** on the weekend, when we go out in nature and get our shoes caked with mud and dirt.*

Literally: "week-end"!)

週 This kanji means "week." It has the "walk" radical 辶 on the left, poetically suggesting time passing as if on swift feet. The phonetic on the right side of the kanji contributed to the meaning by originally showing concentric circles, suggesting the cyclical nature of time.

末 This kanji shows a tree (木) with the top horizontal line representing a long branch at the top end of the tree.

sora 空 / そら sky

*It's a beautiful sight to see birds **soar** through the sky.*

空 This kanji literally means "empty," as in the kanji compound 空手 "karate," which literally means "empty hands." The kanji has the "cave" radical on top, consisting of a roof with eaves, with the two slanted lines below the roof showing the concavity of the cave. The phonetic is 工, which shows a carpenter's rule for drawing straight lines, with the vertical line in the middle being the handle.

sore それ that (one)

*Hope you're not **sore** about that!*

soto 外 / そと outside

*I always park my De**Soto** automobile outside, since I don't have a garage.*

外 The kanji shows the crescent moon on the left and cracks in a tortoise shell on the right. In ancient China, future events were predicted by burning a tortoise shell to see where the cracks formed. For the divination to be reliable, this had to be done outside of the nighttime hours when the moon was in the sky.

subarashii すばらしい wonderful; terrific

***Subaru**, **she** tells me, makes wonderful cars.*

sugoi すごい awesome; terrific

***Sigourney** Weaver is an awesome actress!*

suki 好き / すき like

*In winter many of us like to **ski**.*

好 The kanji has the "woman" radical 女 on the left and the kanji for "child" on the right. Women, especially mothers, like children.

sukoshi 少し / すこし a little

*Sometimes you can only **squeeze** a little juice out of a lemon.*

少 The kanji shows a slice being taken out of something already small (小), leaving only a little bit of it.

suteki すてき fantastic; terrific

A fine steak (ステーキ) is pretty fantastic!

tabemasu 食べます / たべます eat

*To eat in a civilized way, one **must** sit at the **table**.*

食　The kanji shows a hand on top reaching into a rice bowl in the middle and scooping up the rice with a spoon, pictured on the bottom.

tabun 多分 / たぶん probably

*We humans are probably remotely related to the **baboon**, according to Darwin.*

Literally: "greater-part."

多　This kanji means "many; a lot." It's composed of two crescent moons, reminiscent of the phrase "many moons ago."

分　This kanji as a verb means "to divide," but as a noun means "part." It shows a knife (刀) dividing something up by cutting it into two parts (八).

tachimasu 立ちます / たちます stand

*When you're sitting down having a conversation with someone and they suddenly get **touchy** about something you say, they will very likely stand up and storm out of the room.*

立　The kanji shows a person standing. The top stroke is the head, the top horizontal line the arms, the two slanted vertical lines the legs, and the bottom line the ground.

taihen 大変 / たいへん greatly; awful; tough

***Thai hens** are awfully tough, and therefore rarely if ever used at KFC.*

Literally: "big-changes."

大　This kanji means "big." It shows a person with his or her arms outstretched: "How big was that fish that got away?!"

変　This kanji means "change." The radical on the bottom shows two hands, in this case acting to change something. The top part looks like a person standing straight with arms held defiantly to either side, determined to change something. This top part is actually a simplification after WWII in both Japan and mainland China of what was really a phonetic in the traditional kanji, 變. This original kanji has the "speech" radical 言 in between two silkworm cocoons. Perhaps this phonetic was even intended to contribute to the meaning, since silkworms undergo an amazing change from caterpillar to chrysalis to moth, and because people's words are often so changeable.

The fact that the word for "awful" in Japanese, 大変, literally means "big changes" will have greater and greater significance to you as you grow older, since the older you get, the more you find any changes awful and tough to accept.

taitei たいてい usually; generally

*English gentlemen generally wear a **tie** for afternoon **tea**.*

takai 高い / たかい expensive; high; tall

*Sometimes **tacky** things can still be expensive.*

高 The kanji shows a two-story building. The two small boxes represent the upstairs and downstairs windows, with a roof on top. Originally the kanji just meant "tall; high," but in time came to also mean "high in price," i.e., "expensive."

tako タコ octopus

Be aware that when you order a tako in a Japanese restaurant, you will be served octopus rather than the Mexican taco you might crave.

tame ni 為に / ために for the sake of ...

For the sake of ***Tommy****, and especially for the sake of* ***Tommy's knees****, his hockey coach gave his goalie, Tommy, extra thick knee pads.*

為 According to the 2nd-century Chinese etymological text *Shuowen Jiezi*, the kanji shows a mother monkey with one fore-paw raised above her head. Below her forepaw is her head and breast. Her feet are on the very bottom. The explanation is that the mother monkey does a great deal for the sake of her child, just as a human mother does.

tanoshii 楽しい / たのしい pleasant; enjoyable; fun

Tan? Oh, she *finds that most enjoyable out on the beach.*

楽 The kanji is a simplification of the traditional kanji 樂 for "music; joy" still used in Taiwan and Hong Kong and by Chinese in the West. It shows two bells surrounding a drum on top, placed on a platform made of wood (木), which constituted ancient Chinese music. Music is a great source of enjoyment, said Confucius, so this kanji also came to mean "enjoyable; pleasurable" when not in combination with other kanji. The simplification in modern Japanese replaces the bells on either side of the drum with what appear to be sound waves emanating from the drum.

tatoeba 例えば / たとえば for example

There are many things that older people in the U.S. don't understand about the younger generation. ***Tattoos of a*** *strange figure, for example.*

例 The kanji has the "person" radical 亻 on the left, since we humans look to great people as examples to follow. The phonetic on the right has the "death" radical 歹 on the left, which depicts a skull, and the "sword" radical 刂 on the right.

There are certainly many examples in Shakespeare's plays of characters dying at the hands of a knife or sword.

tazuneru 尋ねる / たずねる visit

*I would like to visit **Tanzania** and do a safari.*

尋 The original meaning of the kanji, which it still retains in Chinese, is "search; seek." It's composed of four radicals. It has a hand on top (彐), reaching out for something. Below the hand is a carpenter's rule (工) and a mouth (口). Since the carpenter's rule represents "work" in kanji, think about how we all search for work, as we make verbal requests (口) to employers. The very bottom of this kanji has another way to depict the hand (寸), which shows the thumb and forefinger and again emphasizes the idea of searching. When we seek to visit someone or some place, we need to search them out.

tegami 手紙 / てがみ letter

*Rather than asking our friends to write us a letter, on Facebook we often just say to them, "**tag me**!"*

Literally: "hand-paper."

手 This kanji means "hand." The three horizontal lines represent three of the fingers on a hand, with the vertical line representing the wrist.

紙 This kanji means "paper." It has the "thread" radical 糸 on the left, since early Chinese writing was on silk before paper was invented. The phonetic on the right shows a water plant, stretching out its tendrils. Perhaps it was chosen over other possible phonetics because when we write a letter to someone we are reaching out to them through the medium of written words, much like the water plant reaching out with its shoots. However, in remembering the kanji 紙 you might think of the right side as showing someone sitting at a desk writing a letter, with one foot extended at the bottom right.

And since the "thread" radical looks a bit like a Christmas tree, think of how Christmas time is the season of the year when we are most likely to write letters to those we love.

teinei 丁寧 / ていねい polite

*Polite gentlemen, when declining a cup of tea, will say "**Tea**? **Nay**, but I thank thee."*

丁 This kanji means "nail; tack." It's a picture of a nail, with the head on top and with the vertical line and the small hook depicting the nail's length and the sharp point at the end. For mnemonic purposes, think of it as a small table at which the polite person gracefully sits.

寧 This kanji means "peace." It shows the "roof" radical 宀 on top, below which is the "heart" radical 心. Beneath that is the "eye" radical 目, turned on its side, with the kanji 丁 for "nail" at the very bottom. For mnemonic purposes, think about the polite person sitting at that table (丁) under the host's roof, glancing (目) around the host's home, and with heartfelt (心) graciousness politely complimenting the host.

These two kanji were only used to transliterate the Japanese word into Chinese characters and do not reflect the meaning.

tekitoo 適当 / てきとう appropriate; suitable

*To get the appropriate fit for the customer's shoes and ensure a suitable size, the skilled shoe salesperson seizes the measuring tape and **takes it to the toes.***

Literally: "suitable-equal."

適 This kanji means "suitable; appropriate." It has the "walk" radical 辶 on the left. The right side depicts a scholar-official of ancient China, with the top part representing the head and the bottom part a long flowing garment. It originally meant an official who had passed the imperial examinations for posting to whichever prefecture or city he was assigned. Since supposedly only qualified individuals would be given these government posts, in time the kanji came to mean "suitable; appropriate." To remember the kanji, think of how when you go to a formal event, you must wear the appropriate clothes.

当 This kanji is a recent simplification of the original kanji 當, still used in Taiwan and Hong Kong and by Chinese in the West. The traditional kanji shows a slanted tile roof with an upstairs window, which serves as the phonetic 尚. The radical on the bottom is the "field" radical 田. The original meaning was "to pawn" your land to get cash. It was borrowed for its sound to mean a number of things in Chinese, and in the case of Japanese serves as a rather arbitrary suffix in 適当. The simplified form 当 of this kanji has always looked to me like the head of a turkey, which is a most suitable dish for a Thanksgiving dinner.

ten 点 / てん score; grade; point

*A perfect **ten** on a scale of 1–10 is an excellent score!*

The kanji as it is now written in Japan and China since WWII is a simplification of the original kanji 點, which has the character 黑, meaning "black," on the left side. The character for "black" shows a window blackened by soot from a fire, indicated by the "fire" radical 灬 on the bottom, on a house made from mud brick, symbolized by the character for "earth" 土. The right side of 點 is the phonetic 占, which shows the cracks in a tortoise shell on top, with the mouth of a soothsayer on the bottom, and means "to foretell the future." The true etymology of this character has to do with the original meaning, which it still retains, of lighting a fire. By extension it came to mean the little bits that are left of whatever is burned by a fire, and by extension "points," and finally, based on the "points" you accumulate, a "grade" or "score." The top of the kanji as it is now written (点) looks a bit like a cigarette lighter being lit, as indicated by the "fire" radical 灬 below it.

tomaru 止まる / とまる stop

*My eating sweets will stop **tomorrow**, I often promise myself.*

止 The kanji shows the foot at rest, with the bottom stroke depicting the sole of the foot pressed flat against the ground and stopped there.

tonari となり next to

*The **toenail** is next to the toe.*

tori 鳥 / とり bird

*Birds like to perch on a **tree**.*

鳥 The kanji shows the crest on top of the head of a bird like the Asian magpie or the North American cardinal. The four small strokes on the bottom of the kanji represent the tail feathers, with the strokes in the middle of the kanji representing the body and wings of the bird.

toru 取る / とる take

__Thor__ will take his hammer to send a thunderbolt at his enemy.

取 The kanji shows a hand on the right (又) taking hold of someone by the ear (耳).

totemo とても very

*A **totem** pole is very tall.*

ude 腕 / うで arm(s)

My underarms exude a lot of odor!

腕 On the left of the kanji is the "meat" radical ⺝, which appears in all the kanji for fleshy body parts including arms, legs, chest, and back. Although scribes made this radical look exactly like the kanji 月 for "moon" when they codified the language several thousand years ago, it's a distortion of the kanji 肉 for "meat." The right side of the kanji (宛) is only there as a phonetic, but it looks like two people sitting back to back under a roof, not using their arms, since they seem to be resting.

undoo 運動 / うんどう exercise; sports

Exercise is no fun when your ***undoo-wear's*** *(underwear's) tight!*

Literally: "transport-move."

運 This kanji, which means "to transport," has the "walk" radical ⻌ on the left, indicating movement. The phonetic on the right shows a wheeled vehicle (車) under a roof and means "military." Soldiers in the military are ordered to do a lot of exercise, whether in boot camp or on the march in battle. For us civilians, when our car is under the roof of our garage and not working, we are forced to get exercise by walking instead.

動 This kanji means "to move." It has the "energy" radical 力 on the right, with the kanji 重 for "heavy" on the left as the phonetic. 重 shows weights piled up, as they would be at a gym. The idea is that you use a lot of energy to move something heavy.

unten (suru) 運転 (する) / うんてん(する) (to) drive

*A race car driver might say to himself, as he drives in a race and goes to shift gears, "**Um, ten** speeds would be even better than five!"*

Literally: "transport-drive." Often used with *suru*.

運　This kanji, which means "to transport," has the "walk" radical ⻌ on the left, indicating movement. The phonetic on the right contributes to the meaning by showing a wheeled vehicle (車) under a roof.

転　This kanji, which means "to drive," has the "cart" radical 車 on the left. The simplified phonetic on the right has the kanji for "two" above a pictograph showing a nose. Think of it as the nose of a child trying to see out over a side window of a car.

urayamashii　うらやましい　envious

*In the Bible, King David was envious that **Uriah** the Hittite had a beautiful wife, Bathsheba, whom he desired for himself, and so decided that **Uriah must** die.*

ureshii　嬉しい / うれしい　happy

***Hooray**, I'm so happy that she loves me!*

嬉　The kanji has the "woman" radical 女 on the left, whose presence so often brings happiness to children. The phonetic 喜 on the right side by itself means "joy." It seems to show 11 (10 + 1) mouths on top and 20 mouths on the bottom, representing a great many people eating, drinking, and singing happily at a party. That is actually not too different from the true etymology of the character. The character on the bottom does show a great many mouths happily drinking and singing at a celebration. The top part, however, actually shows the head of a drum being beaten in time to the joyous singing at the party.

ushiro 後ろ / うしろ back; behind

*My wife and I like to sit far from the screen when we go to the movies, so they always **usher** us to the back **row**.*

後 The kanji shows the "step" radical 彳 on the left, appearing to depict one person behind another. It is actually a footprint. The right side shows two hands on the bottom dragging behind a string or rope, represented by the "short thread" radical 幺 on top.

wakai 若い / わかい young

*Young children adore the Muppets character, Fozzie Bear, who often says "**Waka! Waka!**"*

若 The kanji has the "grass/flower" radical 艹 on top, referring to young plants or grasses just beginning to grow. The phonetic below it is the kanji 右 that means "right," (as opposed to "left"). 右 depicts the right hand feeding the mouth, since all Asians traditionally have been taught to eat with their right hand, to prevent righties and lefties ever bumping elbows at the table. In remembering the kanji 若 think of what the poet e.e. cummings said, namely that "for whenever men are right, they are not young."

wake わけ reason; explanation

*There must be a reason why we sometimes **wake** up in the middle of the night in a cold sweat.*

yasai 野菜 / やさい vegetables

*The vegetables served in school cafeterias tend to be so tasteless, that students often lament to each other "**yeah, sigh**, vegetables again!"*

Literally: "wild-vegetables."

野　This kanji means "wild." The meaningful part is on the left, which combines the "field" radical 田 with the "earth/ground" radical 土. The land outside of the cultivated fields was "wild," i.e., uncultivated. The phonetic on the right is the pictograph of a spear and was meant only to serve as a phonetic. However, in remembering the kanji it might help to think of wild, uncivilized tribes using spears rather than more modern weapons for hunting.

菜　This kanji means "vegetables." On top is the "grass/flower" radical 艹, which is the radical on top of a great many characters for various vegetables, as well as kanji for flowers and herbs. Beneath it is a phonetic that seems to show a hand pulling out a plant from the ground, like a carrot or turnip, although here it is the "tree" radical 木.

yasashii　易しい / やさしい　easy

Yes, sir, she *can do it easy (easily).*

易　The kanji shows the head and four legs of a chameleon. It originally meant "to change," since the chameleon changes its coloring to blend in with the environment. In time, however, the kanji came to mean "easy," since the chameleon so easily changes its skin color.

yasui　安い / やすい　cheap

Yeah*, chop* ***suey*** *is cheap.*

安　The kanji shows a woman (女) under a roof. The original meaning of this kanji, which it still retains in both Chinese and Japanese, is "peace," since the woman is safely ensconced at home. However, in the past century this kanji when used by itself came to mean "cheap" in Japanese. As a feminist, I am embarrassed to say that my mnemonic device for this is that when your wife is at home, she can't spend your money. Of course she likely has a computer, a phone, and credit cards, so she can buy plenty of expensive stuff from home!

yasumi 休み / やすみ rest; break; holiday

***Yeah, sue me**, but I'm taking a break!*

休 The kanji shows a person on the left resting under a tree (木).

yoru 夜 / よる night

*"Alas, poor **Yorick**, he's died and gone into that great night we call death," Shakespeare's Hamlet might have said.*

夜 The kanji shows a person on the bottom left under a roof at night, with the moon shining in on the bottom right (a variation of 月), which almost appears to be walking into the room!

yubi 指 / ゆび finger

*My Mom would point at me with her index finger and say, "**You be** a good boy now!"*

指 The kanji has the "hand" radical 扌 on the left, appropriately enough. The phonetic on the right, which contributes to the meaning, shows a finger on the top sticking something tasty in the mouth, seen on the bottom of the character. When the ancient Chinese scribes codified the language several thousand years ago, they made the mouth filled with talk or with food look (日) exactly like the pictograph 日 for "sun."

yubiwa 指輪 / ゆびわ ring

*When I proposed to my wife, I put a diamond ring on her finger and said "**You be wan**-derful! Please marry me!"*

Literally: "finger-ring."

指 The kanji has the "hand" radical 扌 on the left, appropriately enough. The phonetic on the right, which contributes to the meaning, shows a finger on the top sticking something tasty in the mouth, seen on the bottom of the character. When the ancient Chinese scribes codified the language several thousand years ago, they made the mouth filled with talk or with food (曰) look exactly like the pictograph 日 for "sun."

輪 This kanji means "ring." It has the "cart" radical 車 on the left, giving a bird's-eye view of a wheeled vehicle in which the two horizontal lines represent the wheels, the vertical line the axle, and the middle box the body of the cart. The idea here is that a ring is round, like the wheels of a cart or carriage. The phonetic on the right represents a written document in ancient times, composed of slats of bamboo tied together vertically (冊) and placed under a roof. A helpful mnemonic might be to think of a wedding being legalized by the giving of a ring and a written marriage certificate.

yuki 雪 / ゆき snow

*As beautiful as snow can be, when we have to drive in it, we may say "**yuck**!"*

雪 The kanji has the "rain" radical on top (雨), which is found on the top of all kanji having to do with weather. The top line of the "rain" radical shows the sky, with the straight horizontal and vertical lines below representing a cloud from which raindrops are falling, as depicted by the four small slanted lines. To create this kanji, on the bottom a hand (ヨ) is added to show the act of brushing away the snow.

yume 夢 / ゆめ dream

You may *have just been dreaming.*

夢 This kanji has the "grass/flower" radical 艹 on top of the kanji 目 for "eye," turned on its side. At the bottom is a pictograph of a roof, underneath which the moon (夕) can be seen shining in. The idea here seems to be that as you sleep under your roof at night with the moon visible in the sky, flowery visions appear before your eyes. That is close to the true etymology, which is that the "grass/flower" radical on the top was a distortion of the ancient kanji that was intended to show the eyes beclouded in sleep and therefore seeing things rather indistinctly in one's dreams.

yunomi 湯飲み / ゆのみ teacup

*"**You know me**, I love tea" say your Japanese friends, when you ask them what they'd like to drink.*

Literally: "hot water-drinking."

湯 This kanji means "hot water." It has the "water" radical 氵 on the left, appropriately enough. The phonetic on the right shows the sun on top shooting its rays down to the earth, contributing to the idea of heating the water.

飲 The kanji has the "food" radical 食 on the left, which shows a hand on top reaching into a rice bowl in the middle and scooping up the rice with a spoon, pictured on the bottom. The right side shows a person on the bottom, with breath rising up, and means "to inhale." When we drink, it is often with food, and we figuratively inhale the beverage.

yuube 夕べ / ゆうべ last night

***You, babe**, were so fun last night!*

夕 The kanji shows the crescent moon appearing in the sky in the evening.

yuubinkyoku 郵便局 / ゆうびんきょく post office

*"Have **you been** to the post office today?" the boss asked her.*

Literally: "postal-convenience-station."

郵 This kanji means "postal." It has the "city wall" radical ⻏ on the right, which is the outline of the building blocks of a city wall. The phonetic on the left side shows hanging plants, but looks a bit like letters piled up at the post office.

便 This kanji means "convenient." It has the "person" radical 亻 on the left, since we humans are always looking for more convenient ways to do things. The right side shows a messenger striding along (吏) carrying a bundle or package of some kind. It's certainly more convenient to have someone else carry a heavy burden for you than to do it yourself.

局 This kanji means "office; station." Although it is written with the "corpse" radical 尸, it should be thought of as the "doorway" radical 户 since the top stroke was accidentally omitted when the kanji was codified several millennia ago. The phonetic 句 at the bottom by itself means "phrase" and shows breath emanating from a mouth. This seems an appropriate choice of a phonetic, since so much talk goes on in offices.

yuugata 夕方 / ゆうがた evening

You gotta *have fun in the evening, if you work during the day.*

Literally: "moon-place."

夕 This kanji depicts the crescent moon and is a variation of the kanji 月 for "moon." It is never used by itself but appears in certain kanji compounds and as a radical.

方 This kanji means "place." It looks like a square boat lashed to the shore. Since the boat is tied to the shore at a certain location, it came to mean "place." According to the 2nd-century Chinese etymological text *Shuowen Jiezi*, it may well be a deliberate distortion of the Buddhist "swastika" (卍), which symbolizes that God is everywhere and in every place, north, south, east, west, above, and below.

yuujin 友人 / ゆうじん friend

*I have a friend named **Eugene** in **Eugene**, Oregon.*

Literally "friend-person." Formal for *tomodachi.*

友 This kanji means "friend." It appears to show one hand (ナ) grasping another person's hand (又) in friendship. However, according to the 2nd-century Chinese etymological text *Shuowen Jiezi*, it shows the hands of friends working together toward some mutual goal.

人 This kanji means "person." It depicts human beings as two-legged creatures, as opposed to horses, cows, etc., which walk around on four legs.

INDEX

activities, *katsudoo,* 活動 / かつどう, 50
again, *mata,* また, 62
air, *kuuki,* 空気 / くうき, 59
airplane, *hikooki,* 飛行機 / ひこうき, 34
all; everyone, *mina,* 皆 / みな, 63
animal(s), *doobutsu,* 動物 / どうぶつ, 24
another, *hoka,* 他 / ほか, 35
answer, *kotae,* 答え / こたえ, 57
appetite, *shokuyoku,* 食欲 / しょくよく, 91
apple, *ringo,* りんご, 77
appropriate; suitable, *tekitoo,* 適当 / てきとう, 103
arm(s), *ude,* 腕 / うで, 106
awesome; terrific, *sugoi,* すごい, 98

back; behind, *ushiro,* 後ろ / うしろ, 108
bad/poor at something, *heta,* 下手 / へた, 33
bag; book bag; backpack, *kaban,* かばん, 43
be surprised, *odoroku,* 驚く / おどろく, 71
beans; peas, *mame,* 豆 / まめ, 61
bedroom, *shinshitsu,* 寝室 / しんしつ, 89
(to) begin, *hajimeru,* 始める / はじめる, 30
beginning, *hajime,* 初め / はじめ, 29
bicycle, *jitensha,* 自転車 / じてんしゃ, 41
bird, *tori,* 鳥 / とり, 105
blue, *aoi,* 青い / あおい, 14
body, *karada,* 体 / からだ, 47
book(s), *hon,* 本 / ほん, 36
borrow; rent, *kariru,* 借りる / かりる, 48
bride, *shinpu,* 新婦 / しんぷ, 88
business trip, *shutchoo,* 出張 / しゅっちょう, 96
business, *shoobai,* 商売 / しょうばい, 92
buy, *kau,* 買う / かう, 51

cap; hat, *booshi,* 帽子 / ぼうし, 18
car, *kuruma,* 車 / くるま, 59
cat, *neko,* 猫 / ねこ, 68
Catholic priest, *shinpu,* 神父 / しんぷ, 88
chair, *isu,* 椅 / いす, 38
chat; talk, *shaberu,* しゃべる, 84
cheap, *yasui,* 安い / やすい, 109
chopsticks, *ohashi,* お箸 / おはし, 72
coffee house, *kissaten,* 喫茶店 / きっさてん, 56
cold (the virus), *kaze,* 風邪 / かぜ, 51
cold (air temperature), *samui,* 寒い / さむい, 78
common; usual; ordinary, *futsuu,* 普通 / ふつう, 27
company, *kaisha,* 会社 / かいしゃ, 44

complaint, *monku,* 文句 / もんく, 65
convenient, *benri,* 便利 / べんり, 17
corner, *kado,* 角 / かど, 43
culture, *bunka,* 文化 / ぶんか, 18
custom; habit, *shuukan,* 習慣 / しゅうかん, 96

dance, *odoru,* 踊る / おどる, 71
dark, *kurai,* 暗い / くらい, 58
diarrhea, *geri,* 下痢 / げり, 28
dictionary, *jisho,* 辞書 / じしょ, 40
difficult; hard, *muzukashii,* 難しい / むずかしい, 66
direction, *hoomen,* 方面 / ほうめん, 35
dirty, *kitanai,* 汚い / きたない, 57
discovery, *hakken,* 発見 / はっけん, 30
dislike, *kirai,* 嫌い / きらい, 55
do, *shimasu,* します, 87
doctor, *isha,* 医者 / いしゃ, 37
dream, *yume,* 夢 / ゆめ, 111
drink, *nomimasu,* 飲みます / のみます, 70
(to) drive, *unten (suru),* 運転 (する) / うんてん(する), 106

ear, *mimi,* 耳 / みみ, 63
easy, *yasashii,* 易しい / やさしい, 109
eat, *tabemasu,* 食べます / たべます, 98
empty, *karappo,* 空っぽ / からっぽ, 47
English language, *eigo,* 英語 / えいご, 25
envious, *urayamashii,* うらやましい, 107
era; age; period of time, *jidai,* 時代 / じだい, 39
escape, *nigeru,* 逃げる / にげる, 69
etc.; and so forth, *nado,* など, 66
evening, *yuugata,* 夕方 / ゆうがた, 113
examine a patient, *mimasu,* 診ます / みます, 62
example, *rei,* 例 / れい, 76
exercise; sports, *undoo,* 運動 / うんどう, 106
expensive; high; tall, *takai,* 高い / たかい, 100
experience, *keiken,* 経験 / けいけん, 52
explanation, *setsumei,* 説明 / せつめい, 83

face, *kao,* 顔 / かお, 46
fantastic; terrific, *suteki,* すてき, 98
father [honorific], *otoosan,* お父さん / おとうさん, 74
find, *mitsukeru,* 見つける / みつける, 65
fine; just right, *kekkoo,* けっこう, 54
finger, *yubi,* 指 / ゆび, 110
fish, *sakana,* 魚 / さかな, 77
foot/feet, *ashi,* 足 / あし, 15
for example, *tatoeba,* 例えば / たとえば, 101
for the sake of ..., *tame ni,* 為に / ために, 101
free time, *hima,* 暇 / ひま, 34
freedom; free, *jiyuu,* 自由 / じゆう, 41
friend, *yuujin,* 友人 / ゆうじん, 114
front, *mae,* 前 / まえ, 61

game; match, *shiai,* 試合 / しあい, 85
get angry, *okoru,* 怒る / おこる, 73
get up, *okiru,* 起きる / おきる, 73
go, *ikimasu,* 行きます / いきます, 37

god; god(s), *kami,* 神 / かみ, 45
good at something; skillful, *joozu,* 上手 / じょうず, 42
government, *seifu,* 政府 / せいふ, 79
grammar, *bunpoo,* 文法 / ぶんぽう, 19
grandfather [honorific]; grandpa, *ojiisan,* おじいさん, 72
grandmother [honorific]; grandma, *obaasan,* おばあさん, 70
greatly; awful; tough, *taihen,* 大変 / たいへん, 99

happy, *ureshii,* 嬉しい / うれしい, 107
he; him, *kare,* 彼 / かれ, 48
head, *atama,* 頭 / あたま, 16
here, *koko,* ここ, 57
hobby, *shumi,* 趣味 / しゅみ, 95
homework, *shukudai,* 宿題 / しゅくだい, 94
hospital, *byooin,* 病院 / びょういん, 19
husband, *danna,* だんな, 23
husband and wife, *fuufu,* 夫婦 / ふうふ, 27

I (humbly) receive, *itadakimasu,* 頂きます / いただきます, 39
increasingly, *masumasu,* ますます, 62
injury, *kega,* けが, 52
inside, *naka,* 中 / なか, 67
introduction, *shookai,* 紹介 / しょうかい, 92
island, *shima,* 島 / しま, 87

job; work, *shigoto,* 仕事 / しごと, 86

last night, *yuube,* 夕べ / ゆうべ, 112
laundry, *sentaku,* 洗濯 / せんたく, 83
learn; remember; memorize, *oboeru,* 覚える / おぼえる, 70
learn; study, *manabu,* 学ぶ / まなぶ, 61
lend, *kasu,* 貸す / かす, 49
letter, *tegami,* 手紙 / てがみ, 102
like, *suki,* 好き / すき, 98
a little ... [adverb], *chotto,* ちょっと, 21
a little, *sukoshi,* 少し / すこし, 98
location; place, *basho,* 場所 / ばしょ, 17
lose (something), *nakusu,* なくす, 67
love, *ai,* 愛 / あい, 14
lunch, *chuushoku,* 昼食 / ちゅうしょく, 22

marriage, *kekkon,* 結婚 / けっこん, 53
meat, *niku,* 肉 / にく, 69
medicine, *kusuri,* 薬 / くすり, 59
(to) meet, *au,* 会う / あう, 16
method; way, *hoohoo,* 方法 / ほうほう, 36
minute, *fun,* 分 / ふん, 26
money, *okane,* お金 / おかね, 73
morning, *asa,* 朝 / あさ, 15
mother [honorific], *okaasan,* お母さん / おかあさん, 72
mouth, *kuchi,* 口 / くち, 58
my mother [humble], *haha,* 母 / はは, 29
my father [humble], *chichi,* ちち, 20
my husband [humble], *otto,* 夫 / おっと, 75
my parents [humble], *oya,* 親 / おや, 75
my wife [humble], *kanai,* 家内 / かない, 45

narrow, *semai,* 狭い / せまい, 81

near; close, *chikai,* 近い / ちかい, 21
neighborhood, *kinjo,* 近所 / きんじょ, 54
nephew, *oi,* おい, 72
new, *atarashii,* 新しい / あたらしい, 16
newspaper, *shinbun,* 新聞 / しんぶん, 87
next to, *tonari,* となり, 105
niece, *mei,* めい, 62
night, *yoru,* 夜 / よる, 110
novel, *shoosetsu,* 小説 / しょうせつ, 94

O.K.; all right; fine, *daijoobu,* 大丈夫 / だいじょうぶ, 22
octopus, *tako,* タコ, 100
of course, *mochiron,* もちろん, 65
old, *furui,* 古い / ふるい, 26
older brother [honorific], *oniisan,* お兄さん / おにいさん, 74
older sister [honorific], *oneesan,* お姉さん / おねえさん, 73
oppose, *hantai,* 反対 / はんたい, 31
order (something), *chuumon,* 注文 / ちゅうもん, 21
outside, *soto,* 外 / そと, 97

painful, *itai,* 痛い / いたい, 39
pay, *harau,* 払う / はらう, 31
person, *kata,* 方 / かた, 50
photograph, *shashin,* 写真 / しゃしん, 84
plate; dish, *sara,* 皿 / さら, 79
play a string instrument, *hikimasu,* 弾きます / ひきます, 33
pleasant; enjoyable; fun, *tanoshii,* 楽しい / たのしい, 101
poem, *shi,* 詩 / し, 85
polite, *teinei,* 丁寧 / ていねい, 103
politics, *seiji,* 政治 / せいじ, 79
poor, *binboo,* 貧乏 / びんぼう, 18
post office, *yuubinkyoku,* 郵便局 / ゆうびんきょく, 112
pot, *nabe,* 鍋 / なべ, 66
practice, *renshuu,* 練習 / れんしゅう, 76
praise, *homeru,* ほめる, 35
preparation, *junbi,* 準備 / じゅんび, 43
pretty; clean, *kirei,* きれい, 56
probably, *tabun,* 多分 / たぶん, 99

quarrel, *kenka,* けんか, 54
question, *shitsumon,* 質問 / しつもん, 90

rain, *ame,* 雨 / あめ, 14
reason; explanation, *wake,* わけ, 108
relatively; fairly, *kanari,* かなり, 45
relatives, *shinseki,* 親戚 / しんせき, 89
rest; break; holiday, *yasumi,* 休み / やすみ, 110
result, *kekka,* 結果 / けっか, 52
ring, *yubiwa,* 指輪 / ゆびわ, 110
room, *heya,* 部屋 / へや, 33
rudeness, *shitsurei,* 失礼 / しつれい, 91

sad; lonely, *sabishii,* 寂しい / さびしい, 77
scary; frightening, *kowai,* 怖い / こわい, 57
school, *gakkoo,* 学校 / がっこう, 27
score; grade; point, *ten,* 点 / てん, 104
seat, *seki,* 席 / せき, 81

see, *miru,* 見る / みる, 64
she; her, *kanojo,* 彼女 / かのじょ, 45
short (in length), *mijikai,* 短い / みじかい, 62
should, *beki da,* べきだ, 17
sick; ill, *byooki,* 病気 / びょうき, 20
simple, *kantan,* 簡単 / かんたん, 46
singer, *kashu,* 歌手 / かしゅ, 49
sky, *sora,* 空 / そら, 97
sleep, *nemasu,* 寝ます / ねます, 68
slow; late, *osoi,* 遅い / おそい, 74
small; little, *chiisai,* 小さい / ちいさい, 21
snow, *yuki,* 雪 / ゆき, 111
soap, *sekken,* せっけん, 81
society, *shakai,* 社会 / しゃかい, 84
south, *minami,* 南 / みなみ, 63
speak, *hanashimasu,* 話します / はなします, 30
specialty, *senmon,* 専門 / せんもん, 81
spicy; hot, *karai,* 辛い / からい, 47
spring, *haru,* 春 / はる, 31
stand, *tachimasu,* 立ちます / たちます, 99
star, *hoshi,* 星 / ほし, 36
stay/live somewhere, *kurasu,* 暮らす / くらす, 58
stop, *tomaru,* 止まる / とまる, 105
store, *mise,* 店 / みせ, 64
store, *shooten,* 商店 / しょうてん, 94
strange, *hen,* 変 / へん, 32
summer, *natsu,* 夏 / なつ, 68
swim, *oyogimasu,* 泳ぎます / およぎます, 75

take, *toru,* 取る / とる, 105
tea, *ocha,* お茶 / おちゃ, 71
teacher, *sensei,* 先生 / せんせい, 82
teacup, *yunomi,* 湯飲み / ゆのみ, 112
telephone, *denwa,* 電話 / でんわ, 23
test, *shiken,* 試験 / しけん, 86
that (one), *sore,* それ, 97
the future, *shoorai,* 将来 / しょうらい, 93
thick; fat, *futoi,* ふとい, 26
thief, *doroboo,* どろぼう, 25
this (one), *kore,* これ, 57
throat, *nodo,* のど, 69
ticket, *kippu,* 切符 / きっぷ, 55
today, *kyoo,* 今日 / きょう, 60
tomorrow, *ashita,* 明日 / あした, 15
tooth, *ha,* 歯 / は, 29
town, *machi,* 町 / まち, 60
train/subway station, *eki,* 駅 / えき, 25
treat to food or drink, *ogoru,* おごる, 72

ugly, *minikui,* 醜い / みにくい, 64
umbrella, *kasa,* 傘 / かさ, 48
under; below, *shita,* 下 / した, 90
usually; generally, *taitei,* たいてい, 100

vegetables, *yasai,* 野菜 / やさい, 108
very, *totemo,* とても, 105
view, *nagame,* 眺め / ながめ, 67
visit, *tazuneru,* 尋ねる / たずねる, 102

walk, *sanpo,* 散歩 / さんぽ, 78
want; desire (something), *hoshii,* 欲しい / ほしい, 37
war, *sensoo,* 戦争 / せんそう, 82
(to) wash, *arau,* 洗う / あらう, 15
water, *mizu,* 水 / みず, 65

weekend, *shuumatsu,* 週末 / しゅうまつ, 97
west, *nishi,* 西 / にし, 69
what?, *nani,* 何 / なに, 67
when?, *itsu,* いつ, 39
white, *shiroi,* 白い / しろい, 90
who?, *donata,* どなた, 24
who?, *dare,* 誰 / だれ, 23
why?, *naze,* なぜ, 68
win, *katsu,* かつ, 50
woman; female, *josei,* 女性 / じょせい, 42
wonderful; terrific, *subarashii,* すばらしい, 98
work, *hataraku,* 働く / はたらく, 32
world, *sekai,* 世界 / せかい, 80
write, *kakimasu,* 書きます / かきます, 44

years of age, *sai,* 歳 / さい, 77
yesterday, *kinoo,* 昨日 / きのう, 54
you, *anata,* あなた, 14
young, *wakai,* 若い / わかい, 108
younger brother [humble], *otooto,* 弟 / おとうと, 74
younger sister [humble], *imooto,* 妹 / いもうと, 37
"you're welcome," *doo itashimashite,* どういたしまして, 24

CHART OF RADICALS

	1 STROKE	
1	一	one
	丨	line
	丶	dot
	丿	bend
5	乙 (乚)	second
6	亅	hook
	2 STROKES	
7	二	two
	亠	lid
9	人 (亻, 𠆢)	person
	儿	legs
	入 (𠆢)	enter
	八 (丷)	eight
	冂	inverted box
	冖	cover
	冫	ice
	几	desk
	凵	open box
18	刀 (刂, ⺈)	sword
	力	energy
	勹	wrap
	匕	spoon
22	匚	box frame
23	匸 (匚)	hiding
24	十	ten
25	卜 (⺊)	divination
26	卩 (㔾)	seal
27	厂	cliff
28	厶	nose
29	又	right hand
	3 STROKES	
30	口	mouth
31	囗	enclosure
32	土	earth
33	士	scholar
34	夂	double hands
35	夊	winter variant
36	夕	evening
37	大	big
38	女	woman
39	子	child
40	宀	roof
41	寸	inch
42	小 (⺌, ⺍)	small
43	尢 (尣, 允)	lame
44	尸	corpse
45	屮	sprout

46	山	mountain
47	巛 (川, 巜)	river
48	工	carpenter's rule
49	已 (己,巳)	self
50	巾	turban
51	干	dry
52	幺	short thread
53	广	roof with wall
54	廴	long stride
55	廾	twenty
56	弋	dart
57	弓	bow
58	彐 (彑)	pig's head
59	彡	hair
60	彳	step
	4 STROKES	
61	心 (忄, 㣺)	heart
62	戈	halberd
63	戶 (戸, 户)	doorway
64	手 (扌, 龵)	hand
65	支	branch
66	攵 (攴)	strike
67	文	script
68	斗	dipper
69	斤	axe
70	方	square
71	无 (旡)	crooked heaven
72	日	sun
73	曰	say
74	月 (⺝)	moon
75	木	tree
76	欠	lack
77	止	stop
78	歹 (歺)	death
79	殳	weapon
80	毋 (母)	mother
81	比	compare
82	毛	hair
83	氏	clan
84	气	steam
85	水 (氵, 氺)	water
86	火 (灬)	fire
87	爪 (爫, ⺤, ⺥)	claw
88	父	father
89	爻	mix
90	爿 (丬)	left side
91	片	right side
92	牙	tooth
93	牛 (牜, ⺧)	cow
94	犬 (犭)	dog; animal
95	玄	dark
96	王 (玉, ⺩, 𤣩)	king
97	瓜	melon

5 STROKES		
98	瓦	tile
99	甘	sweet
00	生	life
101	用 (甩)	use
02	田	field
03	疋 (⺪)	cloth
04	疒	sickness
0	癶	footsteps
10	白	white
107	皮	skin
108	皿	dish
09	目	eye
10	矛	spear
11	矢	arrow
112	石	stone
13	示 (⺭)	god
14	禸	track
1	禾	grain
116	穴	cave
117	立	stand
6 STROKES		
118	竹 (⺮)	bamboo
19	米	rice
20	糸 (糹)	thread
21	缶	pottery
122	罒 (网, ⺳,罒)	net
123	羊 (⺶, ⺷)	sheep
124	羽	feather
125	耂 (老, 耂)	old
126	而	rake
127	耒	plow
128	耳	ear
129	聿 (⺻)	brush
130	肉 (⺼,月)	meat
131	臣	minister
132	自	self
133	至	arrive
134	臼	mortar
135	舌	tongue
136	舛	opposite
137	舟	boat
138	艮	stopping
139	色	color
140	艹 (艸, 龷)	grass; flower
141	虍	tiger
142	虫	insect
143	血	blood
144	行	go
145	衣 (衤)	clothes
146	西 (襾, 覀)	west
7 STROKES		
147	見	see
148	角	horn
149	言 (訁)	speech
150	谷	valley
151	豆	bean

52	豕	pig
53	豸	cat
54	貝	shell; money
55	赤	red
156	走 (赱, 走)	run
57	足 (⻊)	foot
58	身	body
59	車	cart
60	辛	spicy
61	辰	morning
162	⻌ (辵, ⻍)	walk
63	邑 (阝)	town; city wall
64	酉	alcohol
65	釆	divide
166	里	village
8 STROKES		
167	金 (釒)	gold; metal
68	長 (镸)	long
69	門	gate
70	阜 (阝)	mound
71	隶	slave
172	隹	short-tailed bird
73	雨 (⻗)	rain
74	青 (靑)	green
175	非	wrong
9 STROKES		
176	面 (靣)	face
77	革	leather
178	韋	tanned leather
179	韭	leek
180	音	sound
181	頁	head
182	風 (⺇)	wind
183	飛	fly
184	食 (飠)	food
185	首	neck
186	香	fragrant
10 STROKES		
187	馬	horse
188	骨	bone
189	高 (髙)	tall
190	髟	hair
191	鬥	fight
192	鬯	herbs
193	鬲	tripod
194	鬼	demon
11 STROKES		
195	魚	fish
196	鳥	bird
197	鹵	salt
198	鹿	deer
199	麦 (麥)	wheat
200	麻	hemp
12 STROKES		
201	黄 (黃)	yellow
202	黍	millet
203	黒 (黑)	black
204	黹	embroidery

13 STROKES		
205	黽	frog
206	鼎	kettle
207	鼓	drum
208	鼠	rat
14 STROKES		
209	鼻	nose
210	齊	even
15–17 STROKES		
211	歯 (齒)	tooth
212	竜 (龍)	dragon
213	亀 (龜)	turtle
214	龠	flute

VOCABULARY NOTES

VOCABULARY NOTES

Other Titles of Interest
from Stone Bridge Press
www.stonebridge.com

BOOKS BY LARRY HERZBERG AND QIN XUE HERZBERG

Speak and Read Chinese: Fun Mnemonic Devices for Remembering Chinese Words and Their Tones

Basic Patterns of Chinese Grammar: A Student's Guide to Correct Structures and Common Errors

Chinese Proverbs and Popular Sayings: With Observations on Culture and Language

China Survival Guide: How to Avoid Travel Troubles and Mortifying Mishaps

ADDITIONAL TITLES

Japanese the Manga Way: An Illustrated Guide to Grammar and Structure
by Wayne P. Lammers

Crazy for Kanji: A Student's Guide to the Wonderful World of Japanese Characters
by Eve Kushner

Kanji Box: Japanese Character Collection
by Shogo Oketani and Leza Lowitz

Kanji Pict-o-Graphix: Over 1,000 Japanese Kanji and Kana Mnemonics
by Michael Rowley

Michael Rowley's Kanji Pictographix Dragon Book: Blood, Fire, and Spirit
by Michael Rowley

Kanji Starter (volumes 1 and 2)
by Daiki Kusuya

Japaneseness: A Guide to Values and Virtues
by Yoji Yamakuse

Womansword: What Japanese Words Say About Women
by Kittredge Cherry